Raw Gold

A Spiritual Experience Through Schizophrenia

A Collection of Poems
by
Robin Millhouse

First published in Australia in 2021 by Robin Millhouse

Edited by Tracey Regan – All Things Writing

© Robin Millhouse 2021

All rights reserved. No part of this book may be used or reproduced by any means, graphic, electronic or mechanical, including photocopying, recording, taping or by any information storage or retrieval system without the w ritten permission of the copyright owner.

ISBN : 978-0-6453666-0-0

CONTENTS

INTRODUCTION 1

CHAPTER 1 3
    MONKEYING WITH MY SOUL.................................5
    HERALDING A NEW ORDER..................................12
    VISIONS OF A LIFE ETERNAL.................................13
    PLEASURE DOMES AND PALACES OF ICE..............14
    THE HOLY THREE...15
    THE RISEN STAR..16
    KNOWING MY DESTINY 17
    THE WHORE OF THE SOUTH...................................18
    EARTH GODDESS 19
    LAKE OF DESIRE 20
    DONE IT..21
    WON IT 22
    UNKNOWN RACES...23
    ORANGUTANG..24
    ENLIGHTENMENT 25

CHAPTER 2 27
- PLEASING MYSELF 29
- POEM TO PLEASE MYSELF 33
- MY CUP RUNNETH OVER......................................34
- JOY IN THE MAKING 35
- TRIPLE JOY 36
- ABUNDANCE...37
- CROWN LAW 38
- DUALITY'S PRICE 39
- CREEDS UNKNOWN 40
- BLESS MY SOUL 41
- ROMAN HERESY 42
- TIDINGS OF JOY 43
- SEVEN CRAZY TUNES 44
- DOG ROSES 45
- DREAMING OF BURIED ROSES..............................46
- FATHER..47
- LOVING SIMPLY 48
- THE FLAME OF LIFE 49
- CANDLE VISIONS 50
- THE BURNING BUSH 51

CHAPTER 3 53
- BUCKING NIGHTS AND ROARING DAYS 55
- VISIONS OF A NEW WORLD ORDER......................63
- VASES AND OTHER SYMBOLS...............................64
- TIME TRAVEL..65
- A THORNY PATH...66

ROSE PETALS 67
PINK PRAYERS 68
IN PREPARATION 69
PLAY TIME 70
MOON DRENCHED, I GREET THE SUN 71
DORMOUSE MUSINGS ON PRIDE 72
AMBER THE PUSSY CAT 73

CHAPTER 4 75

CRYSTAL PALACES 77
AMETHYST THRONES 85
ALIGNING MYSELF WITH MARS 86
COMET TALES 87
WORKING DAY WISHES 88
ONE HUNDRED AND ONE DAYS 89
LEEWARD TO THE SIDE OF DEATH 90
ICE BATTLEMENTS 91
LEONINE 92
BIRTHING STARS 93
EXCALIBER 94
THE CHICKEN AND THE EGG 95

CHAPTER 5 97

THE SHAPE CHANGERS 99
A BONE TO PICK 104
HARPING ON PLEASURE 107
TEARS OF GOLD 109
GOLDEN APPLE 110

PEARLS TO SOW IN A PIG'S SILKEN EAR	111
NIGHT WORK	112
FOR GORDON	113
DOLDRUMS	114
THE DREAMING	115
ZEN ON TOAST	116
DRACUNCULAS NIGHT	117
RIVEN GOLD (MARK 1)	119
RIVEN GOLD (MARK 2)	120

CHAPTER 6 121

BLUE HORSES IN PARKS OF BLUE ROSES	123
KINGS AND QUEENS OF OLDEN TIMES	130
VICES I NEVER KNEW I HAD	131
WILD HORSES	132
LARKING IN THE PARK	133
CHILD OF FLESH	134
RETURNING A DAUGHTER TO HERSELF	135
LULLABY	136
NOT GUILTY	137
THE RAVISHED QUEEN	138
COFFEE ANYONE?	139
GOLDEN CHARIOT	140
LOVE'S FULFILMENT	141
MY DESIRING HEART	142
EGG TOKENS	143
NEW-LAID EGGS	144
RHYMES OF AN ANCIENT	145

CHAPTER 7 147
- BRIGHT BLUE WHALES 149
- SONS AND DAUGHTERS OF DEATH 155
- BLUE HUMPED WHALES..157
- SUMMER PALACES 158
- ANNUAL GENERAL MEETING OF WHALES 159
- BIRTH OF SUMMER WHALES 160
- AWAITING BIRTH..161
- BEACHED WHALES..162
- DOLPHINS AND WHALES..163
- WHALES, AND OTHER HEAVY LUMBERERS 164
- DREAMING DONKEYS 165
- SLINGING A SLANGER 166
- FREEDOM TO FIGHT 167
- GIVING IT UP FOR LENT..171
- LYING TONGUES...173
- BLEATING THE LAMB 174
- LOVES TRAFFIC IN THE DARK....................................175
- A RISEN NEW CHRIST 177
- RETURNED CHILDREN 178

CHAPTER 8 179
- FRIENDS AND OTHER FELONS 180
- THE WHITE BALLOON (MARK 1)................................185
- THE WHITE BALLOON (MARK 2)................................186
- CHRYSALIS..187
- DESERT SANDS 188
- HUNGER OF MY HEART (MARK 1) 189

HUNGER OF MY HEART (MARK2) 190
COMET ROCK 192

CHAPTER 9 193
HAVING NO REGRETS 195
THE MAD JACK-UPPER OF ROSE TREES 201
PRESENTS FROM HELL 205
HEALTH: A PRESENT FROM HELL 207
HAPPINESS ALWAYS BEGINS AT HOME 208
HAIR 209
ALICE 210
CONCRETE JUNGLES, AND OTHER PARKLANDS 211

CHAPTER 10 213
PLEASANT WALKS IN THE BLUE PARK 215
PLEASING THE MANY BY PLEASING THE FEW 221
RADIANT WATER 222
CETATION DREAMS 223
VISIONS SEEN IN A CUP OF TEA 224
I MUST HAVE FAITH IN THE PROCESS OF MY REBIRTH. 225
PLAYING A WAITING GAME 226
APPLE BLOSSOM PAIRS 227
LOVE SONG TO MYSELF AND A SINGING WHALE 229

CHAPTER 11 231
ROSE-COLOURED FACETS 233
GRIEF I USED TO HUG BUT NOW HOLD SACRED 238
OSSIE EMU AND HIS CRICKET TEAM (MARK 1) 239

OSSIE EMU AND HIS CRICKET TEAM (MARK 2)	244
OSSIE EMU AND HIS CRICKET TEAM (MARK 3)	249
MY PATE ON A PLATTER	253
THE UNKNOWN MAN	254
THE SPORT OF KINGS	255
TALES TO TELL MOTHER	256
BALD PATES AND SAVAGE FELINES	257
SONG OF DEATH	258

CHAPTER 12 259

OPENING MY ARMS TO BLUE HORSES	261
AMAZING AMAZONS	265
LONG LIVE THE QUEENS	266
GEORGINA AND THE WHITE ANTS (MARK 1)	267
GEORGINA AND THE WHITE ANTS (MARK 2)	269
FOR GEORGINA	270
GEORGINA THE GREEN	271

CHAPTER 13 273

BLUE SPIRIT POLES AND OTHER ART WORKS	275
REAPING HAVOC'S HARVEST	279
PALACE RELIEF	281
A RIPPING GOOD TIME	282
THORNY TOAD	283
REPTILE BRIDES	284
MUSINGS ON LOVE	285
THE INS AND OUTS OF LOVE	286
SUBSONIC GRIEF (MARK 1)	287

SUBSONIC GRIEF (MARK 2) 288
DOG STAR VISIONS 289
LITTLE GIRL LOST 290
BREAKING THE SEALS 291

ABOUT THE AUTHOR 295

INTRODUCTION

Raw Gold is my spiritual experience through schizophrenia. It is a collection of poems, mainly channeled work, although some of the writing is my own, as is the clarification of some of its obscurity. It may be of interest to readers experiencing spiritual growth, those who enjoy poetry, or have a curiosity around schizophrenia.

It is the story of a woman in her mid-forties who, after leaving home when her marriage ended, experienced schizophrenia, which played a part in how she worked with clients when using the modality 'Touch for Health'. (Touch for Health, now more commonly called Kinesiology, uses muscle testing to get answers from the body's inner intelligence.) The book dwells on new relationships with men and sadness over losing her husband and daughter.

In the book, Ra is a spirit entity who largely took over my life and played a part in my spiritual alteration during the time I was 'within the belly of the whale.' My spiritual experience certainly wasn't orthodox and it was strange taking down hundreds of poems which came to me like dictation. It was also unexpected when my body could be directed and moved in accordance with what was needed during my Kinesiology sessions.

After thirty-two years, my life is much improved, including living with schizophrenia.

Regards,
Robin.

CHAPTER 1

MONKEYING WITH MY SOUL

'No gorilla is going to monkey around with my soul,'
she said, eating Danish pastry and drinking chamomile tea.
I sat between two marys who visited me in hell's kitchen
and, speaking of souls and monkeys, Margot
(the first of three marys who would visit me that day)
quoth truly, but not with any knowledge
concerning matters arising from hell,
or of this maze of animals which I call my menagerie.
Having been hit by schizophrenia and feigning death
the night before my friends arrived,
I was betrayed (so says my host)
by one called Judas Iscariot - Karen, that is -
who visited me that morning. Blaming myselves,
(believing I was indeed inhabited by ghosts,)
I espied a way to die yet once again.
Giving Judas a kiss, I betrayed Karen
with two pieces of silver, and climbed upon a bed
strewn with petals, which roses never blessed.
Having no desire, I lay beneath my unsuspecting client,
who, playing Judas, rose again as Karen.
Then foully possessed in the spirit of Jesus I arose
and offered her the water of life,
dying once more then before her eyes.
Giving myself the benefit of the doubting Thomas
she was proving to be, I never doubted

I would rise (or wise up) to things now hinted
which one day would come true.
The three marys, finding the tombstone rolled away
that afternoon, entered to find their friend
not quite gone mad, yet barely seeming to be.
Truly gladdened by their presence, I trained
my mystical eye upon the first mary, Margot - she who spoke
of monkeys and souls, and monkeyed around her chair,
hissing like a snake. Devilish dreams
are not always what they seem, and appearances
never quite show the truth. Having been
within the whale's belly now for nearly half my term,
(before sliding into dreams and illusions
lost to mankind's vision,) I crave the love of He
who loves me most of all, and bless the day
I was found mad, though alive, by Jill, my third mary.
She combed my hair and, holding me to her breast,
seemed to mother me to death. Calling me 'sun,'
she dried my tears and cried my cries, whaling
away times when she and her nice new husband, Jim,
delighted in calling one another names -
which hardly suits the game of love they play.
Having no desire to participate in the exorcism game
they later tried to make me play, I played a role
to satisfy them - but not myself ...
Yet concerning she who combed my hair and summonsed
    me up a tree
to monkey around with her soul, I praise Jill now

for not weeping as one bereft,
for I raised myself up in her love.
The three marys who found me gone away did not like it
when I returned to tell new lies.
Joking thus, I monkeyed with their souls
a little longer than I ought,
for having died upon a cross the night before
to bear up worldly grief alone,
I craved the love of friends
who now crave their former friend's return.
Rings of fire and ice surround the four of us
as we separately travel paths unknown. Belatedly
I blew myself to bits of heart and bone,
when recently chewing over certain ghosts who commonly
blow dust in eyes, and finger moons in skies unknown.
Braving new worlds, I dry my eyes upon a thorn,
and now blow raspberries which grow up taller than beanstalks
which my friends and clients climb to stars unknowing,
to doggedly face giants who hack down trees of wrath.
Yes - only spiritual pathways plot races, so pacing hearts
stolen from queen's tables of riven gold.
Nowadays I am driven on and always up
to look upon the light of suns and blazing stars
which never formerly were mine. However, now that I
bake new-laid tarts which savour of heaven-sent
new-laid eggs, I am no longer driven
to do much more than the good lord needs.
Creeds which blab of the new world order

and greater glories than I've ever known
are driven before my eyes in chariots of fire,
and beg me now not to stop at gates
(unless inlaid with pearls.)
In monkeying with my soul, the whale who mothers me
sends messages from hell to others now -
when formerly it was only I
who received such telegrams. Having been thrice-blessed,
I now bless others, and write epistles
which sting like nettles, and grow horny spikes
which prick and tear at other eyes.
Bating bears and lions in the park
of He who whips but scorns us not at all,
I line up paper tigers to play parts in my menagerie.
Ra, Tiger Burning Bright and Sheer Khan
are really no more than Amber the pussy cat
(who is myself,) dancing and dreaming her way
to monkey up trees where roses spread their unique petals
to perfume gardens. Dreaming in parks unknown,
the cats and I play away our days,
dressed up to kill the common herd with love.
So, through monkeying with my soul, He
who plays the lark and whistles souls to death
has praised me higher than a dog-star dressed in drag.
Rose garden queens who bake tarts to tether souls
monkey with their own souls-
thus biting the spoon which fed them.
Glory be to spoons which feed monkeys

who, climbing down from high perches,
preach to others that which only they have taught themselves.
Concerning my second mary, Lucy - she who brought
sweetened chickpeas to the feast in hell's kitchen
and terrified herself by monkeying around a tree of her own,
(the tree of which I speak offers fruit
to whet appetites, and drive dragons
to dry tears of gold - the dragons
being none other than myselves, who wear their hats
wryly over their ears, seeing that whales
and other creatures now bless themselves daily
and dry eyes which never cried tears of gold -
(or any other metal for that matter,)
unbelievers like Lucy - as well as Margot and Jill -
never toe depths of unknown deeps.
Only my Judas, Karen, who that morning I betrayed
with a hiding wrapped up as a kiss,
conducted herself well in the eyes of my ghosts.
She never budged when, bludgeoned half to death,
I died before her eyes a number of times
before she upped and left me high and dry-eyed
upon the cross which fate flew in the face most foully.
Crying rivers of gold, I brought myself to bear
the cross alone. Draining myself dry, I blew my rosy nose
and played up later than I believed was possible.
When my grieving friends brought flowers and fruit
(hoping, perhaps, to torture away ghouls and goblins?)
I never died that chattering hissing death again,

nor weighed upon their souls - as they did mine.
I merely disagreed that I was mad.
Finding me thus gone again, Jill brought
crystals, cape and candle to my flat
and, wrapped in a doona,
I peacefully bore their pot-luck bible exorcism.
I even followed them home for a cup of tea
just so they could see I was capable of driving the car.
When they were satisfied I was none other
than the bird they'd always known, I slipped off home.
But do not take it amiss when I say
that a bird in hell's kitchen fumes dragonly breath
unless allowed to choose her ghouls and ghostly friends.
Lucy, though graven on my heart,
told tales of madness to my mum - reasonably so, I own,
as lately my cattery has got me claiming
to be goddess, queen of tarts,
who sends heavenly flavoursome souls to stages unknown
by chariots of fire which haul after them the wrath of ages.
Lucy, bless her, has borne me up many times
when cakes from hell's kitchen have burned my mouth.
Margot and Jill helped too in whistling this romance
upon legs stronger than granite -
which stones other beasts burdening my menagerie
to bits of heart and bony chalk.
The chalk of which I talk, Gordon and Rachael
are much estranged since the humble burning days
of my marriage. I left them long ago

and whole once more, no longer humbled
by those I love more than they know,
I dream of days when once more we may fly up on roofs
to perch and crow of times before I entered
the whale's belly - or played upon a lute.
Having left my former perch, I while away
the hours in writing verses
which hardly rhyme - and reason simply
to those who know me not at all.
But to end this epistle from hell
I'll fire up my dragons, hoping for brighter, better days
when I leave the belly of the whale
by an exit which may prove (so they say) the only way out
for one soon to be praised sky-high.

HERALDING A NEW ORDER

Arising unbidden in the night,
I accept forbidden fruit
ladled to me from dream's kitchen
and returning, catch dog-star visions
of a new order which, heralded
by the Zodiac, staves off threatened wars.
Mars, protecting her ancient herds
directs a fiery sword
towards earth's newly-risen cause,
sending comfort to her who hears the word.
Peace prizes and offerings of bounteous joy
rain down on earth:
gross tidings telling tales
of wondrous victories.
Seeded with prophetic visions,
I take tokens of gold
to share among friends.

VISIONS OF A LIFE ETERNAL

Death, seeking to distract this dream
of life, wears multi-coloured clothes.
Facing multitudinous lives, we span the aeons,
never glimpsing golden pockets
in time's eternal face.
Rolled into balls,
past, present and future time
flows stilly. Moving outwards
from the centre currents radiate
their multi-layered lives.

PLEASURE DOMES AND PALACES OF ICE

A lake of crimson water will soon be lit
by blue-gold rays, showing east and west
their destiny. Chained to a wall, dying
by degrees, inching towards their deaths,
frozen from love's grasp, spirits shout, scream
cry mercy, mercy, mercy to skies
divided by a two-faced god who gives no favour
left or right, but parts the bloody waters
to wash joy and sorrow from the face of both.
Ra, the eternal flame, lunges forward
to fight a gross battle, engendering eternal life.

THE HOLY THREE

Late one night (or early in the morn,)
the evangelicals spake of a blue moon
dawning in an eastern lake, crimson
with blood of the sacrificial lamb.
The three spake to me
saying 'holy, holy, holy,
thou art blessed by the trinity,
and surely will die, die, die to thine own will.'

THE RISEN STAR

Rejoice oh leonine one. Take up
thy sword and burnish thine armour.
Roses grown solely for thee,
spring blooms glistening with dew,
bring fragrant new life.
Planets bursting open across the sky
bear your star
to wondrous new heights.

KNOWING MY DESTINY

Shattered,
knowing wholeness is near,
believing I'm guided towards my destiny,
I accept the gifts of a love
far greater than I've ever known,
and spend my dreaming days
engaged in creation's rebirth.

THE WHORE OF THE SOUTH

Aligning myself with Mars, I caress the hand
which once had scorned my pleas for aid
against a plague of fleas. Ant hills,
mountainous with hope, house lives
of rapturous ease in southern seas. Breezes
stiff with sand, whisper of a lotus land
where brilliant suns beat golden
upon lazy enemies of time's old trade.
Gallipoli's dying mother, fearing the sword,
faces north and dreams of a crimson rose
whose petals bleed in times of need.

EARTH GODDESS

Mother, the great earth waggyl who slumbers
deep in rivers of dreaming blood,
blows her breath towards the sun.
Enduring crimes destroyers of her sacred soil
(indentured in alien hands) have wrought,
she tolerates the grimy men who spear her side.
Only her death, they say, will ease
their constant fears which, emerging
from undreamed depths, destroy their hopes of love.

LAKE OF DESIRE

Snake and owl, thirsting deep,
desired to drink a dram.
Owl flew up and snake slid down
arriving at the lake together.

Snake, sliding on his belly,
desired water to slake his unquenchable passion.

Owl, flying higher than clouds of unknowing,
needed water, she said,
to grow a multitude of roses.

DONE IT

Having been given keys to visit
the one true god, I never allow any but him
to bark me up trees now I'm mad.

WON IT

Having been given keys to visit
the one true god, I dance to tunes
strumming crazy rhythms in my heart.

UNKNOWN RACES

Having been given keys to visit
the one true god,
I won't be made to play the fool
in spite of cats who plague my days.
But on stormy nights I lie serene
as Ra, Tiger Burning Bright and Sheer Khan
have clowned away my former friends.
So what? On a new moon
there'll be others who'll play hearts to bones.

ORANGUTANG

His soft plate face sags on his chest.
His massive arms hang limp and slack.
Propped, like some forgotten toy,
he watches the barred world stare and leer.
All clumsy kindness, savage jest and jeer
he bears with patience and distain.
He cares no longer, is past the pain.
Indifferent to a life of freedom drained
he's press-ganged into hell's kitchen
to form a right-wing partnership with white owl.
Entering left, snake offers him an apple.

ENLIGHTENMENT

When your appetite for torment
has appeased its every whim,
and you're mentally distracted
and diseased in every limb,
when you're thrown into convulsions
like an epileptic fit
and the blatant bourgeois mutter
there is cause to doubt your wit,
when your heart begins to flutter
wringing sonnets from its pith
and a tongue begins to stutter
there is logic in the myth,
when the veils between illusion
have for you been quickly ripped
and you pass beyond confusion
in a dark and secret crypt,
then a world of wondrous glory
blazes light from seven rays
and, returning, may you beam raw gold
through the brilliance of your days.

CHAPTER 2

PLEASING MYSELF

Pleasing myself, I please the whale who loves me most
of all. Pleasing myself, I also please the three who
please themselves by pleasing me
to bits of heart and bone. Broken bones
and hearts which do not please themselves tell lies and
bite the tails of dragons. They queen it up
in drag to wail away their days with foolish knights.
Having no regrets, I dream up foolish tales
to please myselves and me. We play up
and thus they play the game of life. In winning raw gold
I mustn't deceive myself, or anyone else,
as to the ways of singing whales - and other ghosts.
Having no regrets, I release my former grief
and play upon life's lute to cheer my divided self.
Having no fear that life or death will harm a foolish flea -
or me - I dry the tears of past regrets,
glad I died upon a singing whale
and blew bubbles in bursting breath
which told the fragrance of delicious tarts,
and roses grown in snow. Having no regrets
since entering the belly of the whale,
I praise myself, for unlike the fearful days
when knights slew dragons, and partook of tarts
which stank to high heaven, I now can bless myself
when someone steals my heart. Blowing kisses

in the park, I encourage knights and queens
not to swear oaths decreeing the baking
of those stinking tarts, saying they must
cleanse their hearts with fire.
Having declared war upon stinking roses,
I guide my crew to shores unseen by Gordon
(my dreamy lotus-eating sailor,)
who shows our shrewd perceptive daughter, Rachael,
how to cook creations which pale my cheeks -
yet fill his eyes with tears of joy.
Having no regrets, I please myselves and me.
Loving sailors who crew their crafts
with pleasure-seeking daughters, I now aim
only to please God. That is, I will never please myself
unless I please the three who please me most of all.
Aiming to please everyone, (but most of all myself,)
I please the three who love us all
to bits of heart and bone. Only in loving ourselves to bits,
and taking our bones upon stages of desire
may God's will truly be done. Praise be to the unleavened three
who latterly were one and died upon a cross,
rose upon a thorn, and never scorned
to blow kisses in parks where sleeping brides
awaited unknown grooms. Praise be to her
who, waiting with her candle lit,
hit upon a spark which groomed her
till she also died upon her cross,

and rose to tell the waiting bride stories - to be revealed
only to those who serve
but never wait to see why whales and other creatures
bark their shins - or fins as the case may be -
on crosses which rise in parks where horses
never cross courses, or for that matter,
seas of burning gold. Running courses
for brides who choose grooms of golden burning bushes,
I may never wait again. And now my term
within the whale is half complete, I must teach
my clients only the means of diving deep
within heart and soul to bring up pearls,
which are creamed with loving hearts.
Having just begun to understand the burning bush
which violently shook me up within the whale's belly
the night I died many times, and said
'I am with thee always,' I know now
that the three within and me are never separate.
And as my term is now half empty of kings and queens
who bake wonderful tarts and grow green apples
and golden pears in groves where tigers never prowl,
cats of a different creed (meaning Ra,
Tiger Burning Bright and Sheer Khan ...
and a menagerie of creatures born upon a star)
now wholly fill my mind. Faithfully yours,
we, within the belly of this wondrous whale,
remain your undeserving friend, the one-time critic
who raved of midsummer nights and other plays

where brides like Margot, Lucy and Jill,
priding themselves upon life's stage,
jagged nerves and clawed their way
to greater parts in my desiring heart.
God bless you all, goodnight, goodnight, goodnight.
And from me, the former critic who drank
her dreams to death because in loving the actors
she hated to criticise friends, adieu.

POEM TO PLEASE MYSELF

Pleasing myself, I indulge
a whim for luxury
and witness how serenely
berries hang from trees,
while tigers and lions
claw up some 'treat'
to trick my head.

MY CUP RUNNETH OVER

Pleasure, the means to finding joy,
blossoms devious trust
in crazy tigers and lions,
gleaming their way through forests of fire
to leap constellations in a new world order.
Believing is not seeing
nor is faith a matter of hearing.
Now fish fly in the face of dreams
which one day will come true.
Meandering, I rarely go out nights,
and play away my days at home.
Soon, golden chariots trimmed with blue
will fly me to the moon.

JOY IN THE MAKING

Pleasure, joy's spur,
comes from daily doing
only that within my reach.
Trust (as to why I'm saddled with all this solitude)
reaches out the olive branch.
In teaching others now
I teach myself to trust the day
I died upon a kiss,
rose upon a grief
to die once more the grief of ages past.
Loving others,
I love myself,
and live to breathe the joy
of casting nets wider than hope,
higher than life,
and longer than the reach of man.

TRIPLE JOY

Enforced leisure in a work-ant society
wins the granting of wisdom -
stimulating mental activity,
moral declivity,
and triple-seated liberty.

ABUNDANCE

I reached out for abundance,
never thinking to seek it within.
I need only feel rich to be wealthy;
feeling poor just makes me sad.

CROWN LAW

Arriving late for work,
I find myself joyously employed
in a land where milk and honey
flows unbidden on my desk.
Working for Ra, Tiger Burning Bright
and Sheer Khan, I translate laws
stating that heaven's treasure
lies waiting for those
who regulate their lives.

DUALITY'S PRICE

PLEASURE: Playing the beast of burden,
I ease my days towards the sun.
And having begun to praise a life
I must soon leave,
I bless recurring churlishness.

PAIN: I always do my duty,
and plod steadfast on my way.

PLEASURE: Blessed are the days of peace,
and harmonious evenings of joy.

PAIN: Diseased sailors who go to sea
in leaky vessels,
gain no relief from cankerous sores.

PLEASURE: Blissful are the wages of sin
that claim uneasy hearts
holding secrets.

CREEDS UNKNOWN

Dancing to my own tune now
I'm made to blow my own fanfare,
kiss my own creed,
and desire that dreamy knights
follow me to the ends of the earth.
Brazening out my breath,
I tease disciples
and, awaiting the word,
gird up my tools,
discard my spears,
and joyously await rebirth.

BLESS MY SOUL

Once upon a dew-drop, I learned that roses
were humans in different clothes.
'Old clothes for new,' shouted the pedlar,
so I brought out my trunks of old clobber to swap.
Then, feeling that life had dealt me a raw deal,
I vanished behind a rose bush.
Choosing to regain the scent of snow-grown roses,
I hastened back - parading brand new clothes again.
Glory be to the three on high who raise roses,
and praise be to kings and queens
who, pruning roses, let in light of a brighter sun.

ROMAN HERESY

I am the new Rome, burning to be free
of patriarchy's ancient tree.
From this my broken battlement,
I see winding lines of humbled brides
dancing their way to death.
Believing in the triple-headed God,
I praise the day I died upon a grief
to tear down stony walls.
On rising, I'll raise gold palaces
for those who, living, love.

TIDINGS OF JOY

Preparing for war, suns enfolded in creation's womb
desire a flame to pierce pride
that couples, riding transient waves,
may climb palace stairways to orange groves
within whose succulent fruit
all love resides.

SEVEN CRAZY TUNES

Happiness drives my car
along avenues of golden pear trees,
and blazes my days
through pan pipes of dreams.
Constellations,
created when the womb was young,
draw me by golden strands
to fondly fooling ministers
that my health is great.
Rose tribulations, careering
down laneways lit by Tiger's brightly burning eyes,
close lids to chances which are - not seem -
those that raise lances
and crazily dance
to tangos written out of sync.
Diamond tunes play seven wondrous seals.

DOG ROSES

I dream of spring's bud,
the rising sap of hopes buried in deep snow.
The rose grows silent in the dogwood,
breaking its seals to drip crimson petals
upon the crystalline moon. Rumours of war
herald new-born hope, and stars of the southern sky
blaze a glorious vision of one
who holds Gaia in the folds of her womb.

DREAMING OF BURIED ROSES

Sieving the stream of conscious dreaming,
I awaken to yearnings long buried
in the silt of ancient beds.
Breaking to the surface,
rings of dismal longing
ripple towards banks of golden lands.
Learning that hidden in ancient hills
mysterious groves grow lovely roses,
I drive steep wedges.
A rising perfume
eases the pain of broken sleep.

FATHER

Conceived in God's eye,
I must accept the diamond lotus mystery
which bids I love the whale that mothers me,
the dreaming that grows the one perfect rose,
and the thorn that tears my flesh.

LOVING SIMPLY

Living and loving, I found misery.
Laughing, joying, crazily toying
in present heaven-sent time,
I'm once again in love with life.

THE FLAME OF LIFE

Reaching towards the sun my body eases,
giving itself to love which flows
through rivers tracing out my destiny of joy.

Torn from the monumental flame,
I lost my youthful dream.
Now fire torments my heart again
giving lie to the old belief:
'life's breath is but a little way to death.'

CANDLE VISIONS

Hell's fire and ice-enraging pageant
now pours tepid water on my need to know.
Shoring up my greed for new-born sight,
gods drum crazy rhythms,
torturing sown seed.
Pageants, passing in caverns of the mind,
engage misty wreaths of ethereal wind,
tumbling pre-vision upon pre-vision,
telling of time's new face, written in flame.

THE BURNING BUSH

Cybele, young and beautiful,
acted out her passion.
Pots rose from her fingers,
pans played idylls,
their music sweet as, silently,
she drew her dreams.

CHAPTER 3

BUCKING NIGHTS AND ROARING DAYS

Dreamy-eyed, I meditated on a future time
long past that day I wend my way from beneath
the belly of the whale. Priding myself on having grown
beyond brazening out my breath to wound actors,
I conceived of writing plays and poems -
hoping to please myself, and others.
Then dreaming whalely, I espied one who bagged
my breath, and stole up on me the night I died
a number of times slowly, (but not too agonisingly,)
losing my breath, but not my life -
which surprised me every time I did it.
As I bucked and groaned away the night, he traded
some of my old clothes for new,
and registered my final death in the book of life
as my willingness to wafting away for future lives unknown.
In believing I was dying for the world,
I put my arms around the ball of a tall white vase
and, in switching off the light of my telephone answering
    machine,
had thought my life would instantly be snuffed.
Astounded, I arose knowing I hadn't died at all
at least, not in the usual sense.
Alive but none too well I roared away
the next two hours - or was it four? - time
seems to have escaped me since my deaths,
by means which I was told saved souls. This involved

a kind of bucking, which caused me to groan
and roar like a lion in its death throes.
Yet in dying to itself a lion may not live,
but only lie down to die upon a rose, and rise again
to face another day when Ra, Tiger Burning Bright
and Sheer Khan bless the sky with gold. Once more
I died that day - or was it thrice? I forget.
It hardly matters now, however, as all I want to say
is that in dying to myself yet once again, I traded
a hat of a different tiger to bumble with friends
unwittingly cast in a play. Judas and the three marys
passed my way to say their pieces and play parts
in my burning hell, which houses me now within the
    whale's belly,
where I grow round and fatter than I was.
Greeting my day anew, I brazened out my breath
    once more,
when the three marys, entering my tomb and finding
their friend not there, brazened out their souls,
and wound desiring arms around the one
who only thought she'd gone away. Pleased with myself,
and others who paraded with dreaming whales
and calling cats to flounder in seas of fiery brimstone
and burning ice to tell each other just how lucky
they were in not being up to taking a joke,
or anything at all that looked like wrapping up
such crappy capers as I was offering,
I hoped that they would not be blind to ways

which other travellers to my hell's kitchen
took so lightly, and hastened to explain
the menagerie which framed me.
It was Ra, Tiger Burning Bright and the one called Sheer Khan
who drew me on to pace myself anew,
hissing like a snake at Margot -
which brought me to bear her ire
when she sought to cool my fevered brow with freezing paws.
Gathering up their things, my two marys
left the tomb open for the third,
who combed my hair upon a platter of golden rhyming words.
'Don't give us all that crap about dreaming whales,' she said.
'Cough up and spit out the truth. All those goblins
are no more than hosts of animals.
Ra, Tiger Burning Bright and Sheer Khan are just figments
of a crazed imagination, burning your eyes out in hell.
Brighten up your ideas, Robin Leonie. Pull up your knees
and lighten your load. Strip your platter clean
of filthy cats who claw you where angels fear to prod.'
Having no desire to argue,
I played her game and, combing back my mane, grew wary
of the one I had so recently likened to mother.
Taking on the role myself, I roared her out the door,
and drove myself to even greater depths.

Once more into the dreaming night, I travelled
to distant planets, trying my luck at handing kittens
to unknown cats. Golden daisy-chains, radiating
brilliantly across the miles of planetary gloom,
brought smiles on faces in places unknown,
and races of men and women as yet unknown
greeted my message with joy.
Roses, blooming in a distant spring in unknown groves,
gave their perfume to her who, giving up her ghost
of a chance at ever winning lotto, or running races
against apocalyptic horses, broke rank
and raced away her day in one last roar when learning
that Gyula had failed to keep his appointment in hell's
    kitchen.
Waiting to pounce upon him with gleaming fangs
and friendly paws, Ra brought me to aim darts of fire
down his telephone lines. However, Ra roared that he
    had saved
the day by bringing me another judas - thus pleasing cats
and other animals who poke their noses into business
which stinks to heavens higher than even a white owl
can fly, and longer than a gorilla can reach with both arms
stretched around the world in eighty days,
spent inside the belly of a whale - bursting to rid itself
of one so prickled to death - for happiness came that day
in the shape of Karen. She played the part
that had been reserved for Gyula. Her judas was brilliant!
I only criticised myself as the one

who had roared and bucked herself outdoors.
And, bucking in a final paroxysm of fear,
having sent a glass, spent of the water of life, so it was said,
crashing to the floor, I once more
drew breath to find myself alive - but none too well.
However, Karen never withdrew her hand
from mine - which clutched hers like a straw.
Draining the day's final dregs, I dragged myself to bed
and dreamed of lying beside an angel, who told me
never to raise my eyes to the one called Ra,
unless I waited in the park for paper tigers,
and blew bubbles from things on sticks of burning fire.
She took me to a park that was blanketed with snow,
where roses spread their unique perfume on the frosty air,
and taught me how to blow bubbles of fire. Thanking
the angel for not clawing them to bits, I drew my spear
and pierced my third eye. Only those seared
in kitchens of hell will know that a laser light,
drilling to my brain, brought visions of gleaming cats
and crazy bears and hissing snakes into my line of sight.
Having no idea what pieces are sung by animals
who dance away their hours to unknown tunes, I dreamed
my way into the sun. Remembering what the angel said,
concerning the need to shade my eyes, I saw that I'd lost
sight of what was actually taking place,
by parading ignorantly before the one called judas,
beseeching her to cross her palm with silver.
(This was in fact two silver bags of tea -

bai lin tea, to be precise.) The god
Bai Lin had warned me once never to take him seriously.
I had forgotten this, too, and begging judas to creep
into hell's kitchen on bended knees, I pounced once more
when she returned with the silver tea bags.
Believing she was me, I took away her role as judas
and betrayed her with a kiss. Having only learned
that this meant I was free once more to buck and groan
away my days in hell, I grieved upon a cross,
rose upon a thorn and, picking myself up
from burning floors, faced my friend and blessed her
out the door. Gyula, having phoned me up while I yet lay
agonising on the floor, grew plaintive, and panted to please
me by pouring out sorrows which were at their height.
Relenting, I agreed to see him - but not until
he had cured himself by coming to see me.
My habit had always been to visit Gyula. Many times
he had brought me to his door, and paid my price
for curing his ills, and offering potions and pills
of another kind. Praising the way I'd always raised
his hopes, never dashing his tears away without offering
a paw to lean on, he begged me once more
to come before his door - which soon would open
into jaws of another kind of hell.
When only a week had passed, with it passed also
a part of my menagerie, for beaking and clawing
my way from kitchens of hell in praising Shantha,

Gyula's wife, when she phoned, (speaking in his place
to drum me dancing once more to his tune,) I found
that all but one of the crazed cats, bears, snakes
and other animals had departed for places unknown.
Ra spoke up for Gyula then, proclaiming him king
for more than a day, free from all diseases which previously
had bugged him a lot. I'd had a bugger of a day
and rang bells which summoned up the other cats.
They crawled out of the woodwork, and mewed about a bit
before roaring new commandments. Chastising myself,
I grew grave, and braved Sheer Khan and Tiger Burning
    Bright,
who pounced and once more clawed me to death.
Rising up again, I groaned. All in a day's work now.
I never go anywhere without the three
who rose and fell with me many many many times,
to fill my heart and soul with dreaming whales.
Those crazy cats scream into knights ears, and dream
away queen's tarts by pricking them on to greater virtue
than ever they have known. Now, bucking nights and
    roaring
days away, I while away my time by playing on words,
punning funny rhymes, and never reasoning why
we live and die in so many different ways.
What's the point? When not to know is bliss,
and wisdom sought in caves where bats from hell's kitchen
flutter and bang each other's head to bits of heart
and bone. It preys upon minds as yet unsounded.

Raw Gold

Only in deeps unknown, where hearts unknown
sow minds unknown, can it be said that it is better
by far never to seek to know than learn some truths.
I write away my dreaming mind, and hope to praise
the day when trouble ceases to pursue me. Settlements
as yet unknown from the divorce bring troubles fleeing from
    holes
to shine their blinkered eyes in unknown lights.
Thinking of home and the settlement that is my due,
I wait now nigh on seventeen months to star
in dramas yet untold. But that's another chapter.
See you in the twinkling of a dog's starry eye. Bye.

VISIONS OF A NEW WORLD ORDER

Visionaries, foreseeing my death,
show frenzied pictures in a screaming nightmare
and, dreaming hells of fire and ice,
I tell a dead tale.
Passing through doors marked alphabetically
which offer terrors
I'm shown the infinite light.
Sounds, horrific to my ear, break
from lungs bursting for breath.
Witnessing all, I die for my kin,
suffer sins I do not know,
then blow out a light, believing my own
will instantly be snuffed.
Holding the world in my arms,
I fight for life.

VASES AND OTHER SYMBOLS

My spirit plagued,
I feared losing life.
Able-bodied,
I lost my reason -
finding courage in a vase,
knowledge in a gem
and love in three things:
the whale, myselves and me.

TIME TRAVEL

Flowers budding visions of armoured knights
chained to dragon-dreaming maids
carry images through time and space
of global villages where blue celestial oaks,
pillaged from Jerusalem's token land,
recreate to photosynthesise aquarian love.

A THORNY PATH

Sacred journeyings to planets
prepares my way. Treading paths
smoothed by ancient fishermen
who cast their nets in brimming seas,
I blindly grope my way
midst passion's thorny pride.

ROSE PETALS

Fallen petals of a yellow rose
do not portend sad age.
Pockets in time's dreaming youth,
emptied of bliss, unfold
sagely seed to sow new life.
Heavenly rose,
spill your perfumed petals
of Christ's joy.

PINK PRAYERS

Tributes of camellias array
their glorious pinks
broad-based upon the water,
sending lovely rays to still
the shimmering day's hot breeze.
White buds, dreading winds
which burn their fragile blooms,
move sickly on their tree,
and send grievous messages
to a soul in torment.

IN PREPARATION

Pleasure, pain, fear - or sceptic friends,
won't conquer or deter me.
I am the recipient
of knowledge and wisdom which,
arriving by the Word,
prepared my way.
I am the receiver
of mercy through extirpation.
I am beholden to Christ's flame
whose golden beam now guides me.
I am charmed, entranced, glorified and won.

PLAY TIME

Lou-lou bell, eyes sparkle-bright,
hair frizzed in fright,
arises from night's beaten ring.
Ding-ding-a-ling - hail the new king:
Rex - leonine, golden,
wearing new things, trumpets
of bliss, blows her a kiss,
and departing, prays
for a mistress in hell -
who knows very well
she's sound as a bell,
(Ra, Tiger Burning Bright, Sheer Khan -
all down the well.)

MOON DRENCHED, I GREET THE SUN

Benevolence, beating my breast
like batons of the moon,
weakens my reason, melting
my mind to know its springtime season.
Only bastions of faith, enduring beyond
life's youth glorify the carping tongue
of a winter longing to be free.
Released to autumnal falls
of blown leaves drenched in dew,
my tranquil, undesiring heart expands.
Beaming moons silver my mind
as, smiling, I greet the sun.

DORMOUSE MUSINGS ON PRIDE

Finding the door open,
Ramsay the dormouse scampered silently
through passages in amazing jungles.
He chased tigers
in dark and dreary halls,
catching balls of fire in a golden paw.
Then, maddened by fleas, he scratched
to ease his conscience,
(rubbing raw great patches of pride,)
and buried his heart in stormy seas.
Swallowed by a whale,
the heart was vomited on foreign shores.
Strangers, hearing the wildly beating heart,
mercifully tore it to bits.
The mouse, grown frenzied
without a heart to fill his house,
drove deep wedges in his pride,
took a bride and thus
regained the broken part
which (like Osiris of old,)
mended when Isis
kissed him on both cheeks.

AMBER THE PUSSY CAT

Blissfully seeking new white mice,
Amber the cat stalked silently.
Ears pricked, claws razor-sharp,
she lined her sight against the sun.
Seeing the cat, three white
moon-beam shining mice turned tail
howling their grievance to grandfather clock.
He listened to their story,
then offered sound advice:
'Do not go out at night;
fear death by water;
dread sacrifice by fire.
Darken your light - then Ra,
Tiger Burning Bright and Sheer Khan
will never find you.'
Thanking him profusely, the mice
ran down the clock.
Amber the pussy pounced!

CHAPTER 4

CRYSTAL PALACES

Gyula, finding he had a pain in his kidney,
cried wolf into the jaws
of Sheer Khan, who, climbing upon the table,
roared into Gyula's cups, and greeted him
with a gemstone. Crystal caves and palaces
where fire drains energy from gems, raise Ra
and his crazy cats from dens, to blaze our days
in sunshine. Ra clapped thunderous paws upon Gyula,
firing him up anew when he learned that Shantha
was carrying a child called Freda - who exploded
a bomb in her father's face by claiming she'd
been locked up in the back shed.
Concerning the three who never draw blood,
but only wait for unwary souls
who hide from burning bushes, which shriek
them out of doors to follow their noses
to the stink arising from hell's kitchen
in order to consummate passions unknown, in places
far from home - where Gyula never dares go -
'ra ra ra,' I say for, greening my way, I play
upon stages wrought by Ra. He brews me draughts
in hell's kitchen to ease my ire.
One particularly fiery brew called bai lin
brought me home upon a knight's back, to hack down
poles portending troubled fates, when Freda
called me up on sacred wires. She praised me

when I saved her from a fate worse than knowing
how her father could tell her from the child
he soon would bear, (keeping in mind, of course,
that Shantha, his wife, would be doing the bearing down)
for oats he'd sown would never raise storms
to dry the eyes of dreaming whales, larking it up
in seas of fire. Then laying myself once more
upon the table at Gyula's I offered to cut off
a slice of heart to please the one who Freda
calls her father. Displeased on finding his child
was held prisoner, Gyula cried 'fire and burning brimstone,
where's my host?' at which I returned from tables
where prayers are often said to state the case anew.
Having heard the same old rot about phalluses,
and angels more beautiful than crystal palaces,
I dried my tears once more upon a thorn, and horned
up a nest of trumpets, which played upon his soul
until he died a little to himself. When he'd
emptied his soul of self, I focused my mind
and blew his candle out the back, to light
a burning doll called Rosemary, who'd
been lighting herself up in Gyula's eyes -
destroying his energetic fire. Having placed the doll
of towels on a funeral pyre, Gyula and I heard weeping
and wailing coming from the shed, which stood
backing itself away from the flames.
I summoned up a crazy host of dogs and felons,
who'd been scaring half to death the child, Freda.

So enraged were they by the funeral pyre -
in which they smelt sulphurous flames -
those villains wept and prayed their numbers were not up.
'No vice allowed,' I cried and, taking mercy
on their souls, stoushed them back to hell.
Gyula, relieved of his Rosemary, grew sagacious in time,
and parceled up some items of his own
to throw upon the flames. Then Freda
handed him a package, which set him racing
in unknown parks never to think of pacing himself,
by playing up and tracing female friends -
like the one called Rosemary - who once
had nearly wrung his neck, and blown his candle
well and truly out. Happiness always comes
to he who waits in crystal palaces, and never stares
at female forms which lie upon tables of desire.
I, myself, bore up that table, and carted it away
for cleansing. When it was picked clean of grubs
and other boring things, I wormed my way
around Gyula's little finger to play games
of high treason, and sing ghoulish songs
of things in parks which bark, and stomp
around trees, rooting their truffles in the muck
while trying their luck at lotto, and galloping horses
which run races in parks of pure gold.
Grasping my waist, Gyula flung me on the table.
'I love the way you love and care for me,' he said.
'Jesus wept,' I cried, and dying to myself again,

rose to spear him in the side with thorns
and anything else found lying around.
Hearing myself called by Molly, (my spirit child,)
I braced myself for news of mother, who I thought
was none too well. In fact, I believed her dead.
During my dark night of the soul, I left my bed
and took a candle from the cupboard, lighting it
for the one I love, almost as much as myself.
Placing it beside my bed, I prayed and wept
for she so newly passed away. When morning came,
and I rose to grace the table at Gyula's side,
I heard Molly scream 'mother,
they are dragging me away,' so once again
I dried my eyes upon a thorn and, calling it a day,
relieved myself in Gyula's arms. Recalling
my nightmare lived the night before, I trumpeted
raspberries, telling him how I learned that Molly
was none other than myself in the far-flung
distant future. Then rose-quartz hearts -
which Gyula gave me - fled, leaving truer hearts
to bleed on hearing that races run in spiritual parks
had placed glittering gold in my hands.
I shared my prize with Gyula, and together
we died to ourselves. Locked in arms not truly ours,
we embraced a holy dream, facing ourselves
to rise again like larks - singing songs,
and playing lutes and lyres, a little rusty
from disuse, in parks like the one where Freda

played, before getting herself locked in the back shed
of Gyula's basic desires. Arming myself once more
to trace heraldic faces, I climbed ancient trees,
(in which families root their trusting hearts
and souls,) where only the future stands facing itself.
'Marked down,' cried a voice, proclaiming the sale
of a soul called Freda. 'Half price,' rang out
the voice of Kali, goddess and queen
of Shantha's desiring soul. The price
of Freda's soul was halved, it seems,
because Shantha (a Hindu,) and Gyula (a Christian,)
shared Freda, their child in utero.
Sounds unknown locked Shantha in my arms,
and after tasting sea salt on my lips, I kissed
her forehead, proclaiming the child she bore
was none other than John, the disciple
who wrote Revelations. Shantha, hearing
she was at last with child, wept openly in my arms,
and marked herself as none too blessed by Kali,
who, killing herself in crystalline palaces
of her own making, decreed a death
on undeserving souls who desired Christ for king.
Rowers upon streams of conscious souls froze
when Mark, Gyula's friend, telephoned
to say 'hi,' and, snatching his ear,
bashed it half to death. Caught up in my arms,
Shantha embraced me for the news she was with child,
but Kali, enraged by the loss of one as yet unborn,

Raw Gold

vented her wrath on Shantha, and tore off
strips of flesh. Shantha, growing cold without flesh
to warm her soul, silvered up the golden thing
in a fur of cat. When I lay flurried in a dream
that night, sitting pretty and queening it
with a man called Bob, I was frightened
half to death when a silver cat skittered
straight towards my heart. Finding the kitten
more frightened than myself, I calmed, then saw
it was Shantha, changed into a cat, when wishing
to escape the vengeful Kali - goddess of rage,
who wars against roses, and anything else in her path.
Rising early, I rang Shantha and Gyula to relate
my dream, and offer further word of Freda.
In their days of blooming roses, they awaited
gynaecological confirmation, before relating
the joyful news to Gyula's sister, Eve, who knew
they wanted a child. Eve praised me once
for the way Gyula had fattened from the scrawny youth
he'd been before my healing hands entangled
his sole delight in teasing souls, drawing
out his breath in pastures greener
than a lemon dew-drop to delight his soul -
which grazed away its nights and days,
tucking in Shantha, and dreaming his dreams
of joy and woe. Eve, terrified to bits of heart
and bone by Steve, her lover, threw stones
and blew up bridges she had left uncrossed.

Wending her way to my door, she said, 'massage
my soul, and touch me for health as you do
my brother, for I, too, desire to be well,
now that Steve has torn himself from my side.'
'Righto,' I said, gleaming brightly.
I brazened her body and touched her for health,
so that soon she was well rid of icy hearts
and treacherous urgings which had carried her
so lecherously away. I beamed at her
and touched for health the part that needed
not just burnishing, but replacing by truer metal
than her heart was made of. Dying to myself,
I rose to tell her she was well rid of the one
who had left his mark upon her side. In danger
of icy hearts, and other souls who place themselves
in hands which tear to bits the dreams of those
who tear themselves, I dove again, and rising
with another pearl, craved her shell-like ear
to speak of health, and other things of interest
to one who craved my caring hands.
'Say it out,' she cried, no longer amused
by my wider, and ever-widening circles of words.
I brazened it out: 'He loves you not at all,
and now it's up to you to love yourselves.'
But more of that anon. Ra be with you.
Grace, too. She must never be left from tables
where burning hearts cry creeds unsung.
Later I will sing her songs of love and joy.

Raw Gold

Ta-ta, to-roo and tweedle-dum.
But no, I won't disgrace myself with childish words.
Ta-ta, to-roo and tweedle-dee. Oops,
fiddle-de-dee. Something has gone awry and amiss.
Has anyone seen my face? It's lost
among a load of words. Don't leave me here,
weighed down by blazing swords. Fight for me,
someone. Bear me up. Choose, choose
and choose again to say you love me.
Hearts need flowers, and mine needs roses
to know that it is loved. Here are some for you.
God bless and keep you all. Goodnight.

AMETHYST THRONES

Amethyst thrones, seats of power
for queens and kings, relay messages
of sovereign dowries. Historic pages,
yellowing in ancient bowers,
tell sorry tales of virtue lost.
Queenly visions decry past victories
fought in blood-stained fields
which bear the shame of war.
Astrology, containing prophesies of fire,
rises phoenix-like to dream
new visions of earthly bliss.
Roses, breaking through ash,
will drip their crimson petals
once more on winter gems.

ALIGNING MYSELF WITH MARS

Aligning myself with Mars, I wait upon the will
of one who forces me to bear my lonely heart.
Knowing I must never give my love to those
who shun me, I live now day by day, grateful
for whatever simple kindness comes my way.
The friends who now reject me will find one day
that they desire my love, for I will call
them back when I am changed. But now I wait,
without knowing why I always wait to know.

COMET TALES

Agents of orange, desiring
quick payment bearing fruit,
praise fortitude in one
who bears her grief alone.
Planets shall herald
the birth of a queen,
and stars hasten me to death.

WORKING DAY WISHES

Wishing and shoving my daily bread,
I please noviciates. Singularly,
they ease the aching spirits.
Seeds planted in fertile folds
send roots in search of sustenance,
granting growth. Upturned stones,
grinding out their prototypes,
break sun-baked clay to ripple
urgent, volcanic messages of love.

ONE HUNDRED AND ONE DAYS

A hundred and one days
I have lain in the belly of the whale,
and have witnessed a hundred and one ways
crystalline patterns of ice describe pain.
Penetrating my mind, sunlight
brightens the womb, and bellies forth
words to praise the new-born queen who dies,
rising again to rule.

LEEWARD TO THE SIDE OF DEATH

Having drunk and eaten my fill,
and found life empty, I voided grief.
Dreading all, fearing damnation,
I left home for a mountain-like retreat,
finding not rest, but deeper woe.
Knowing that peace comes
when least expected, my soul
blows freely to the leeward side of death.

ICE BATTLEMENTS

In palace ruins, where bats
cluster in the belfry, I steal
through ancient halls.
Glinting silver, icy shards
from broken battlements
pierce the air with promised peace.
Wending through crazy mazes in my mind
I dream of queens, resplendent
in summer silks, who vanquish
hopeless hordes of war-torn men,
to build again the granary.
Praising the day I died
upon a wish, played
upon a lute, treading
new-made paths to lose and find myself,
I glorify the golden fire
which remelds peace.

LEONINE

Roaring purple oaths, which turn the air
to cobalt blue, I down a cup or two
of amber wine. Dining on golden fish,
(priding myself on devouring portions whole -
a lion's share to bless my ruffled mane,)
I proclaim my royal lore,
and justly tear to tatters
all, who seeking, do not find me leonine.

BIRTHING STARS

Beaming from cataclysmic lives,
constellations sign names in oceans of space.
Cosmic memories of birthing stars
breathe sounding signals
between pinions of staves.
Triumphing across the waves,
the new-born stars gleam palely
into the seeming black of night.
Hearing a cry, I look up.
Though seeing nothing, I know
this sound has travelled light-years
to reach my ear.

EXCALIBER

The cross, rising like Excaliber
from the lake, bequeaths its favour.
Wakened from the pitch of hell,
love guides me from blue shadows
to walk in golden flame.

THE CHICKEN AND THE EGG

The chicken who lays a fine egg,
and numbers it to the peg of a lotto ticket,
gives spiritual gold to her who craves love.
When her life is better than a lemon gum drop,
she'll learn how to enjoy herself,
for only when she blesses herself -
instead of constantly blessing others -
will she taste the sweetness of raw gold.
Then she'll accept the fallacy of false love,
in days when friends could not afford her.

CHAPTER 5

THE SHAPE CHANGERS

Dragons who breathe their fiery breath
upon daughters of fiery fathers, praise the one
who slays the dragon of desire and conjugates words,
urging me on to write of Gyula - a particularly
fiery fella - who belled me yet again, calling me
from hell's kitchen to while away his time and mine,
by sharing a common bone. Shantha, whiling
her time away with a little poppy she was minding,
minded us not when we drew apart, because
she knows her Gyula well. Pleasing ourselves,
we called upon a host of cats who jest,
and ring bells, and drive us into dells unknown -
pleasing themselves by griping away
like hell-bent ghosts. Sunning themselves in parks,
Ra, Tiger Burning Bright and Sheer Khan
play with fire that releases aches in bones.
Gyula and I blew thoughts stating how very deeply
we cared for one another - but as we were both married,
there was no possibility of that! I was married,
it seems, to the one called Gordon. He upped
and left me ... or I upped and left him
I'm not sure which, because neither of us
ever sees the other, which is right because
neither of us loves the other. The reason for this
I'm told by Ra, (my spiritual adviser
in matters of love and war,) is that neither of us

loves ourselves. He says that neither of us
really loves the male and female in us.
'Don't you know it's vital,' said Ra, holding a paw
against the side of his nose, which was itching
because he wanted to sneeze - but dared not
while he was speaking to Gordon and me in the days
when we were married, for then we dwelt
upon the ceiling-level of ourselves, so he blew us
to the floor, that we might ground ourselves.
That was when I opened the door and walked out.
Yes, I remember now - it was me who walked out.
I was studying anatomy and physiology at Tafe,
and attending a boring lecture about blood and bones -
things we all need, but never grow to love.
I remember that I thought someone had vomited,
then found that it was me - sicking up inside myself
because Gordon had said he no longer cared
whether I lived or died upon a rosebush
in parks of dung - which stung to high heaven!
That was when Ra stepped in. Later that evening
when I stepped out the door clutching
an overnight bag in one hand, and a brush and shovel
to sweep up all the dung in the other, Ra,
(seeing that I looked a little lost,) hurried me off
to the one called Kaye. Finding me upon her doorstep,
Kaye baulked somewhat, but asked me in and gave me
tea and sympathy a lot - and a bed which she made up
on her office floor. After rice-cakes for breakfast,

I took myself off to the one called Betsy.
She helped heaps by shoving me on to Jean.
Jean opened her arms to me, calling me 'sister,'
and other sweet names which I forget.
But I do remember it was she who taught me
unconditional love. Jean has a particular talent
for blowing noses in parks of blue roses,
and I love her for it. She mothered me
when I needed a mother most - which is to say
that my own mother, she who reared me
and brought me crayons and paper to draw on
when I was young, but never knew the me
when I grew up and away in my marriage to Gordon ...
what was I saying? Oh yes, the one called Jean
mothered me like an angel, bringing me out of myself,
and offering me her son, Larry, a knight
in common clothing - but a wizard
when it comes to computers. Larry and Jean
once took me to dinner at the Taurus - a steak house
which stank to high heaven, because of the bones
lying about in the kitchen. It wasn't hell's kitchen -
but I'm not too sure because of the stink.
Larry offered me his arm to chew on,
but I refused, preferring the cabbage leaf
on my plate. When I offered him my arm, however,
he leapt on me like one possessed, and gnawed
my arm to the bone, which he then threw
over his shoulder, to join other bones

lying on the floor. He then gnawed his own arm
to the bone, chucking that on the heap
growing visibly before our eyes. When we had consumed
our meal of bloodied meat - noting
that I had refused the meat course, I led Larry
away, and touched him for health in parts
which looked troubled. He didn't like this a bit,
and no more did his mother - because Larry
is the apple of her eye ... which reminds me
of the one called Dorothy. She is my mother-in-law,
but won't be soon, because I will not be married
to Gordon for too much longer. I'm going to marry
the one called Bob. He is the other part of me,
the male side, just as I am the female
side of him - but just because I'm wearing trousers,
it doesn't mean I am a female hiding in male
wolf's clothing - all the tarts these days wear trews.
It's not a bit like days of yore, when damsels
dressed to kill, by dressing up to their eye-balls
in bits of flim-flam, singing their telegrams
to knights who slew dragons, upon wires
which never sang back. Not so these days.
Tarts singing telegrams of love to knights nowadays
are never remiss when they go pop, snap, crackle
upon lines which sink hearts and bones. No go now.
In days of old, knights were more bold, but grew
blue in the face from straining to see
in the telegram whether damsels were in distress

or only distraught because they wore such flimsy
flummery things. What a bummer, I've got to go
and tell Gordon and Larry that I can't
touch them for health - not because they don't
need it a lot - but 'cos they do not like it
when I poke my prying fingers into hearts and bones.
Now here's a bone that you might like to pick.
How would you like it if I touched on
private matters which you'd shoved deep
in your heart and bones? No need to ask.
Just thought that you might like to share my bones.
Ta-ta, goodnight. Happy pickings. Oh, here's someone
who wants a word with me. He just loves bones.
Thanatos is not a nice fellow, but he's not that bad.
Here's a piece about him. Then there's one
that's written by Ra. He's much more charming -
a leonine fellow like myself - or should I say
like Bob? - my male side that loves Ra like myselves,
which is to say I love the three of me -
Ra, and the other two. Well that's
my two bob's worth - for now. To-roo,
see you in a dragon's tear-drop. Don't drop off
to sleep just now, Thanatos wishes to speak -
then Ra will roar it up in parks where dragons
shy away from riderless blue horses.
But that's my next chapter. Bye.

A BONE TO PICK

Significant friends, desiring my success
in matters universal, approached me with care
and enquired whether I'd be needing the bones.
Considering the matter well, I replied
that I would not - so they became the property
of one who chewed them well. Then they were used
for fertiliser. Having no need for fertilised felons,
I let them take the flesh. After that was removed,
I entrusted the spirit to one requiring
the fire of life. And finally, the soul of the matter
went to one who desired a friend. Having given
bones, flesh, spirit and soul,
there remained only a tiny piece of clay.
This, too, was taken
by one who knew me to be generous -
for I willingly gave him my clay
in order to clad a foreign minister's aquarium.
Devoid of life itself, I called
on those possessing the things I'd given
and demanded their return.
They just laughed and called me names.
How long, I wonder, can I live
without bones, flesh, spirit, soul
and the clay that makes me human?
My friends, deciding my gifts weren't worth
their keeping, brought them back.

However, I won't be needing them now.
I died last Tuesday,
was buried Wednesday
and rose again on Thursday.
Please don't think me unfateful,
but I cannot bear to mix
bones, flesh, spirit, soul and clay.
They are tiresome to tote
and cumbersome to carry.
Next time around I won't return
to bear another load.
I'd rather break the seals and stay in hell.
It's a trifle warm in here, but nicer
than the ice room - and much better
than the place where angels, cavorting on clouds
and playing harps, drink tulip wine
and munch on daisy wafers.
Below, my neighbour plays the violin.
Its squeak annoys me a bit,
but otherwise it's comfortable here.
I wouldn't change it for the world -
but if you know a place that's up for sale,
let me know. I don't expect to be here long.
My landlord dislikes his lodgers moving -
however, should you hear of something,
don't hesitate to call. I'm only six feet under
so it won't be any trouble to rise a foot or two.
Hello. Is anybody there?

Did someone speak?
Hey! Does anyone want to share my bones?

HARPING ON PLEASURE

Drinking tulip wine and eating daisy wafers
we while away our days and nights of ease.
Capering upon clouds, we hold our monumental freeze,
and take delight in simple things
which chance to fall our way. Relating
the triumphs of tall boys who died while young
is pleasant work, and by giving strokes and pats
to players in the game of life, we earn
our daily wafers. Peacefully we play our harps
and lyres on clouds spun through with silver,
then sink into the golden sleep of babes.
Rising early, we drink the tulip wine of life,
then stay up late to please our master.
He rises with the sun, then leads his flock
upon a path which lovers choose, never hesitating
to drive his car behind the lesser forms of life.
Wholly sustained in him, we drain ourselves
until we're dry, then drink our tulip wine
to feel refreshed. Thus strengthened,
we wend our way towards night's star,
and gazing on its light, find greater peace.
No privation ever wounds our side,
and only when we blink away the dew, and realign
our lives, do we play once more upon the lute of life.
Unchauffeured cars of white and blue never lose
their way, or stray from paths which mark

our destination, for roses and paths of crazy paving
can't be missed. Upon arrival, we trade
our harps for lutes, and pleasure leads us on
from day to day, right to the journey's end.
In the evening, we ease our aches by fountains
of desire, and when our cups have over-run
at nightfall, we're called back once again.
There, enthralled by pastoral pleasures, we drink
tulip wine, and munch a wafer or three.

TEARS OF GOLD

Two doves I daily feed
leave no crumb to come to grief
among a maze of ancient salt fry.
On nights when rain splashes
tears of gold, and silver softens
cheeks aflame with passions,
I hear a clarion call
which bids me love.
Dragons, drawing chariots of fire
across the sky, breathe flame
which burns the wide-eyed strumpet.
Hearkening to the beat
of her own drum, she cries
riven tear-drops, and dabs
a sodden rag to mop up gold.

GOLDEN APPLE

A better apple, waiting
to be bitten equally in two,
hangs upon a golden bough.
The new-born Adam
gives the fruit to his eventful wife,
entreating her to eat sweet flesh,
ripened to perfection.
Tasting the golden pippin,
Eve breaks with duality,
choosing God's middle way.

PEARLS TO SOW IN A PIG'S SILKEN EAR

Libeling the day's end
I sing the night,
ruing artificial light.
Estranged from the sun,
the evening only just begun,
I submit before the moon
which silvers dreams.
Ancient fisher-folk dive deep,
retrieving pearls
that glow in sunless seas.

NIGHT WORK

Dreaming of work, I tooled up
to deliver the goods.
Creating by day and scheming by night,
I bent my back to hack new paths.
Along the tracks of olden day-dreaming friends,
blackened gorges rise to ram
earth's golden belts to dust.
Home lies yet a long way off.
Cars pass. I never know
whether the driver's friend or foe.

FOR GORDON

As though it was ordained that we should meet
our paths from half the world away did cross,
and, from that chance encounter in the street,
my heart knew love, and cleansed itself of dross.
You stood at least a hero in my sight,
a mountain in a mole-hill race of men:
Hyperion, the sun-god, shining bright,
and I, no titan match, but mere pea-hen.
I know you mortal now. Though not the sun
your light is beacon to me yet, and fire
to meld my scattered several selves to one,
and live in wholeness, free from all desire.
Our paths, once separate, do now entwine.
From yours my light will kindle - both to shine.

DOLDRUMS

No breath or ripple breaks our silvered calm.
Passion spent, we drift and wait.
Entombed in cataclysmic time, we hug private grief,
and neglect the wreckage of our battered craft.
These limp, unmoving tatters we now must mend
or weave a finer sail to catch the wind.

THE DREAMING

Rock ridges, bones of the earth
laboriously bared, provide foundation
for the dreaming. Each root tugged free,
each shovelful of sand removed
helps harden the mental picture:
a house to fit the earth
and best receive the gifts
of light and air. A dream
in rock and wood and glass -
no fantasy superfluous to need
with which to claim 'I have,'
but gracious harmony in statement
of his being: 'I am.'

ZEN ON TOAST

This morning for breakfast
I had zen on toast.
Watching the marmalade
stick in your moustache,
and a dribble of tea dampen
crumbs in your beard,
I drained my cup.
In lightning flash
and thunder of a one-hand clap,
I found my quiddity.
Orange blossom bride
finds marmalade kisses
sometimes give her the pip.

DRACUNCULAS NIGHT

TAKE, POSSESS, LOVE
tears from my abyss.
Desire to ravish
denies the small, still voice.
Dracunculas night, a scream coding silently
ANDROGYNY.
Androgyny, too, has something going for it:
an entity hugging itself.
But goldilocks dionysus
is not my God -
proffering orgy,
tearing the living flesh.
'Not I,' thus sniggered
the little red hen, wearing Nietzche's superman cape.
Dracunculas night
bloodies the pristine moon.
Blowflies buzz
the stinking pistol,
and maggots starve.
Euthanasia has its place
when the cat hungers
but can't eat.
Fly-blown, it is too late.
One wipes the egg-encrusted eye
to appease a nice clean god.
Dracunculas night, women stamp

on Greenham Common:
TAKE, LOVE, USE ME,
howled down by a couple of I Ams.
Dracunculas night, a foetus aborts.

RIVEN GOLD (MARK 1)

Riven gold, arriving later than summer
when fall is overdue, greets my days
with sunshine. Happiness
happens often now. Roses
bless my way, and yet a thorn
impales my heart, for lacking
one true love, I grieve.
Having left my former love
to seek for love's fulfilment,
I now wait riven gold's due date
to heal my heart.

RIVEN GOLD (MARK 2)

You are golden, burning sun,
I, pale moon, pour silver
to cool your heat.
When pride transmutes
we'll find riven gold.

CHAPTER 6

BLUE HORSES IN PARKS OF BLUE ROSES

Having lost my way in a park of blue roses,
I lost my only daughter, Rachael, to her father.
Finding myself in a parkland
where riderless blue horses, urging themselves
back and forwards in time bade me ride,
I grew accustomed to doleful days
spent willing myself towards the time
when Rachael readjusts her mind and opens up
her heart. Realising I'd grown
a most beautiful rose in raising Rachael,
I felt her loss and wept - determining
to build again a peaceful, loving relationship
when she desires it. As a child
Rachael never needed much attention,
because always being good, I could trust
her to do what she was told, and not transgress
rules articulating safety. Food, however,
was a different platter of fish.
At times I thought she'd starve, she ate
so little. Being so very difficult to feed,
I often lost my patience - and when her patience
ran out, she flung runner beans as salt fish
at the wall. When only three, she called herself
recca rachey - appropriate because
throughout her nineteen years while I was home,
she wrecked her bedroom, preferring

disorder and an unmade bed to the discipline
of tidying up her room. Leaving Gordon,
whom I loved more, I thought, than life itself,
felt like stepping out into a vacuum,
that night I packed my toothbrush,
and took myself along to Kaye's - never dreaming
Rachael would slam her mind and heart in my face.
Last November, when returning to collect
my summer clothes, I tried unsuccessfully
to engage her help, so before leaving the house,
said I hoped when she felt better
about our altered situation, she'd come and see me.
'I'll resume my relationship with you,'
she said, 'after settlement.' I wonder
if she realised then it would take so long.
Communication between our family was fine -
as long as things were going well. But whenever
I needed to express unhappiness about
the ever-increasing distance in our lives,
Gordon shrouded himself in silence, disappearing
behind stone walls. Praise be to horses
in parks who never buck riders. Praise, too,
to blue horses in parks of blue roses,
who urge riders towards a life
as glorious as sunrise, harmonious
as the small still voice that sings its bliss
upon a wire, and as sacred and holistic
as power that spirals through the universe,

and turns the helices of DNA.
And praise be to the one who is three -
that is to say Gordon, Rachael and me.
We are only one because we blended our lives
throughout years we lived and loved,
never suspecting the inevitability of parting.
I drank the bitter dregs of sorrow's cup,
but sometimes know that joy which comes
through hell fire's searing.
In parks of blue roses, blue-blooded riders
never need climb back on backs
which buck them off, for their blue horses
are groomed to take their riders towards the sun.
Rachael is none too well these days,
because she never lets her riderless blue horse
within cooee. I, too, am none too well,
because blue-blooded riders are never truly well
until their blood's been drained
by one who loves us most. And as for those
I loved the most - I had to leave them.
I had to learn to love myself, and let
that love ripple out to the whole wide world -
for only when we learn to love ourselves the most,
is it possible for others then to love us in return.
In leaving Gordon, I never intended
rending a chasm between myself and Rachael,
but know that only when she learns
to climb peacefully upon her riderless blue horse,

may we lovingly communicate our hearts.
On the day that pre-trial settlement took place,
Ra raised hell by making me convulse
and roar out truths, which brought guards
running to discover the cause of the racket.
I was taken away by a friendly woman counsellor,
leaving Shirley, my solicitor, to handle the hearing
alone. Before procedures began,
Ra had transferred energies to her
by making me bob up and down.
Knowing I didn't wish to haggle
with one so dearly beloved as Gordon,
he wanted Shirley to carry the case
without my presence in the room.
She stood up for me admirably in this -
in so far as a woman who walks with crutches may.
Shirley's strength is truly magnificent.
She never allows lameness to halt or hinder her
in any way. Having raged Ra's tune
and played a hatter, settlement passed
settling nothing at all for me.
And now that it's too early to get up,
but not too late to sleep some more,
I mustn't forget to tell you of the time
Rachael and I danced in a park at the A.B.C.
The A.B.C. (where I worked - or rather
rattled tea-cups and banged doors in radio plays,)
held socials. Gordon never came, because

he worked ceaselessly. The reason,
it seems, he worked so hard, was because
he never liked picking his bones to learn
why he needed to work harder then other husbands
who could take their wives out dancing,
and enjoy the conviviality of congenial company.
Bored to death by the number of nights
and weekends left alone to my own resources,
I chose learning how to pick bones cleaner
than a postman's whistle - which I miss
these days, as postmen now never blow whistles,
they only blow up storms by delivering
epistles through the post from Gordon,
which tell me of things I'd rather not know -
like how he still doesn't love me,
and that he only wants to know
how we may split up our tables and chairs.
If only he'd known how to divide love
more equably, I'd never have left!
I do not like it on my own. That's why
I won't be on my own much longer
in this particular mountain retreat,
for soon, many riders will come to see me,
and I'll urge them back on backs
which are breaking to receive them.
But now it's up with the lark.
Time to do my tax return. I haven't done it
because of all the poems I've had to write -

or rather, Ra's dictated. At the court
when I was taken away by a lovely counsellor,
she spoke about having certain anxieties
of her own - so I knew she didn't need me
to burden her with all the rumpus
Ra was raging. The noise, I recollect,
was very like that I made at home,
when roaring Rachael out for not wiping up the dishes.
I wonder if she roars at herself
before she'll do them now? She and Gordon
never tell me about their lives - but as I
never tell them about mine, I can't blame Rachael
or, for that matter, Gordon, for never communicating
things they do, because I don't tell them
I don't do the things I seem to -
which doesn't amuse me at all, because
it causes so much trouble! Nowadays,
I go about in not just pairs, but fours.
There's Ra, Tiger Burning Bright - like the one
who burned so brightly in that poem
by William Blake - a riderless horse
who never needed urging on to higher things, because
he did it so well himself. And there's Sheer Khan,
the tigress Rudyard Kipling wrote of
in his jungle book, where animals lived
when the world was younger and greener than now.
The fourth in my menagerie is Amber the pussy.
She's not as sweet as me on a good day,

when the sun is shining, and ginger-carob forthcoming,
but she's not too bad ... in fact
we get on very well, considering I prefer
dogs to cats - but can't have one now
since voiding my rights to live at Sawyers Valley,
where Gordon is building a mansion of stone
called fort Gordo. He calls it that because
he doesn't want people prying around his heart,
to pick his bones. He only likes stones,
maintaining stony silence about matters
concerning his heart. That's why in former days,
when he said 'you have to tell me things
concerning your heart,' we never communicated well.
I always wanted him to intuit my heart,
but whenever it wanted to communicate
he built stone walls, hoping he'd never
have to hear its message. Life's a crumpled rose,
but it won't be too long now before
I'm delivered from beneath the belly
of this whale. How wonderful then,
to see people again. I miss folk very much -
especially Rachael. I hope no one crosses
you off lists as I've been crossed from hers. Bye.

KINGS AND QUEENS OF OLDEN TIMES

Praise be to kings and queens who ride horses
in blue parklands, where no riders wish
themselves backwards in time. Shadows
as yet bridled and bleary-eyed, cast
their nets of silver and gold towards
the setting sun. Only when the day
has ended, and riders rest their heads
once more upon the breasts of blue horses
to urge themselves forwards in time,
will I know my own deep rest.

VICES I NEVER KNEW I HAD

Devices, divorcing me from lovers
lost in blue parks of their own making,
lead me to water horses
where riders throw themselves off
by aligning their fond hopes with Mars.
Riderless horses in blue parks
tease out souls in gold and silver threads,
climbing moonbeams, so riders may remount.
In this glorious new age,
blue horses drink where crosses
bloom like rose trees.
Beneath them, lovers, lost
in each others' arms, rise up again
like larks, to sing the songs,
and play the games,
forever repeating the past.

WILD HORSES

Despairing, the maid paraded her grief
to the river's edge. An ondine
rose before her, saying, 'blue horses,
dragging their riders to drink,
never answer before questions.
Fair daughter of death, curb
your churlish pride, and tether it
to the pole of guidance.'
Ashamed, the maid discarded her robes,
and wholly fearless, left the river.
Turning back the hands of savage time
she straightened her gait,
and rode a blue horse to water the cross.

LARKING IN THE PARK

Larking in the park with one who loves me best,
I swanned up a crow's nest, and adjusted
the angle of my newly feathered friends.
Accustomed now to rising with the lark,
and feeding horses who keep themselves apart
by southern belles and northern stars,
now harkening to my whistle, I place
golden threads between driven wedges
and snow-blown roses, branding myself
as one who blesses horses in bright blue parks.
Having learned to love myself, I never
darken the sun by driving chariots of flame
to turn horses blue, or face courses
other than those which blaze with gold.

CHILD OF FLESH

Piscean virtue, sheathed in steel,
pierces my heart. My daughter's
unrelenting will proclaims
a child grown woman. Beyond my sight
she climbs from stair to star,
seeking cautious passage
through parental tears.
Only in future years may I come to know
what lakes of fire seared her vision,
bringing her up from depths
to honour's blight. Conceived in bliss,
her childish laughter rang a joy which,
culminating through the years, brought
sharp despair to one complacently immured.
My honour now is blighted, too.
Desire of unknown joy has shown
the bankrupt ploys of ancient dreams,
breeding discontent - and bitter wormwood
are the lies upon a child's tongue.
Stars have guided me from child of flesh
to child of spiritual gold, unfolding now
within my womb. I await my legacy of love.

RETURNING A DAUGHTER TO HERSELF

Awaiting a man to waken my dreaming flesh,
I gave myself to one whose full strong beard
grew longest. From early years, our marriage days
were numbered, to burnish golden an unknown son.
Our only daughter, budding from life's burning bush,
shows signs of fainting from the heat of years
which blasted our marriage bed to bits.
Warring roses rise to shake petals of grief
upon her mooning face, which shields its light
from deeper suns - burning to know
why an only begotten daughter dries her father's,
but not her mother's linen, in lines of raging tigers.
Avenues where Simeon peels away his grievous days,
daring myths to write reasons in the snows
of times untrodden, glow glimmering spikes
on trees where no man or woman plods weary on the way.
The sodden sheets, burning upon the tigers' backs,
dry up the years spent longing to be free,
waiting and hoping for a future that will not break
a mother's heart, by parting without saying please.
Awaiting new birth, I ease the pain
by stoppering my pride, and, riding waves of love,
bear unhappiness alone.

LULLABY

Sleep my child, close those heaven-seeing eyes.
Pan pipes to you of golden days,
dreaming just ahead, where laughter brightens
cold palatial halls. Dream my child,
rest your downy head against your mother's breast.

NOT GUILTY

Pleading not guilty,
I raised my face to be kissed.
As no kiss was forthcoming,
I blew out the light.
Chances are I am guilty
of not being the mother
I ought to have been -
but neither is she the daughter
she should be.
Therefore I plead not guilty,
and nor is she.
Whether guilty or not,
I love my daughter,
and she loves me.

THE RAVISHED QUEEN

'I am not guilty,' quoth she, rising
from her dingle-dell. So soundly
did she ring the bell of truth,
it rang the knell of lawyers, who wished
her well on the road to recovery -
following outbursts which sounded
through halls of common lore,
causing anxiety and much alarm.
Knights and ladies swearing oaths rushed in,
carrying away the maid who, all forlorn,
lay spread upon a table of the lawyers -
who wished she would not die on them.
Remembering not to play the fool, she departed
and, teasing them well, lived to play
another day - which is to say that only
by pretending death, do maids brave new worlds.

COFFEE ANYONE?

Afternoon tea, awaited with baited death,
grew cold in the pot, slithered up the spout,
and poured itself out on the floor.
Picking myself off the ceiling,
I ran to the door and cried
'help, the tea is squeezing my life.'
Kinsfolk, who daily drank tea in my parlour,
proclaimed in forked tongues
it was not their fault
if cats had doggerelled my mind.
Solidly set in their creed,
they poured themselves back in the silver
and clanged the lid.
I made myself a cup of coffee,
drinking it straight
from the old cracked pot.

GOLDEN CHARIOT

Traversing golden rivers, I break edicts
of a distant star to battle petty giants.
Seared by a dragon's fiery breath,
my vision clears. The diamond lotus-eyed one
who drives my chariot, cheers me on,
then, beamed from a golden star, I sheath
my sword, knowing glorious peace is won.

LOVE'S FULFILMENT

Ripping free from emotion bonds with Gordon -
following twenty years of a happy marriage -
I let destitution overwhelm and colour my life.
For a time I drifted, aimlessly passing the days,
until conceived and possessed by a blue humped whale.
Now, the longings which formerly obsessed me
have disappeared, as the love I sought
fulfils my life. Despite his daily torments -
which have maddened me to the point of tearing toys
owl, snake and gorilla from their stand -
I love the one who drives me forward,
insisting I push myself to impossible heights.
At times I'm irritated half to death when,
whooshing and shoving, he forces my body
and breath to obey his will. Because I know
he's the only being who truly loves me,
and knows me better than ever lover could,
I choose to accept the divinity he endows,
giving my life to his will.

MY DESIRING HEART

Fearing to lose my heart for nothing,
I gave my love to one who broke my mind.
I lost nothing, nothing at all.
By doing nothing, nothing at all,
time wrought its change,
reshaping me to forge my life anew.

EGG TOKENS

Token eggs, given at Easter,
hatch new life
from out the jaws of death.

NEW-LAID EGGS

New-laid eggs, which steal away desire,
are buried treasure in hearts of fire.
Exiled from my home through disaffection,
I wander now beneath the sky,
and spend my years sagely teasing
silver and golden threads, to braid new love.
Praising the day I rose upon a kiss,
to die upon the cross of roses,
I rise again, and play once more the game of life.

RHYMES OF AN ANCIENT

Myrtle and Daisy, jaunty and crazy,
loving their show-men of straw,
found pleasure abated
and men over-rated
when looking at life in the raw.

Rosey and Lilly, lazy and silly,
laughing their days in the sun,
took to their beds
with pains in their heads
when they ate the forbidden bun.

Bronwyn and Sarah, grooming the bearer
of tidings from god's burning bush,
stray through their days
and never sell bays
to bums steering cars in a rush.

Janice and Mary, always contrary,
finding their friend not at home,
combed out their hair
and discussed how they dare
force love to the limits of a Rome
burning with an unknown passion.

Robin Leonie bought some polony,

feeling the need to eat meat.
She lay down and died
then leapt up and cried
'why croak it, when bread can't be beat.'

Which just goes to prove
it's madness to shove
the wills of the many on one
who, crazy and silly,
drank tea from a billy,
and lay naked beneath a cold sun.

CHAPTER 7

BRIGHT BLUE WHALES

Experiencing sudden weight loss,
I horned myself upon a thorn
until reminded by my host that,
being yet within the whale's belly,
transformation is simply melting a little flab.
Great! It's losing autonomy that really riles me.
My being a kind of foetus
means the whale now chooses my actions -
so I don't go places he desires not,
or have friends he doesn't choose -
but knowing Rex, a former love a little later
than Gordon, stood roaring before my door,
I was able to usher him in.
Having frozen himself from my life,
Gordon doesn't give a fig if I fall in other arms.
He cares no longer for me
now he's got Rachael to care for him.
When Rex came in I shivered up a host
of hell creatures who, rising at my command,
drew his notice to a grieving soul called Rexine.
She dwelt once in a deeper hell
than my hell's kitchen -
and darker by far than the hell
I left at home in leaving Gordon and Rachael
to root for truffles which bored me half to death.
I'm not much good at culinary arts these days

since brewing that stormy dish for Rex.
Praising me the most, he blew out my brains ...
that's in Freedom to Fight,
a poem about stoushing private parts
like hearts and bones. Ra wrote it
while resting his paws. He was licking one a lot
because a thorn was stuck in his pad.
I'm filling up scads of pads these days,
listening in on phones which never ring,
yet still bring messages of hope.
Now I queen it up by larking in my head,
singing like lions ... tigers, I mean -
or is it dreaming whales, blowing bubbles
of thought in my mind? - which is none too well
according to the one called Rexine ...
or is it Rex? He shivered and shook
on learning that his female self, Rexine,
(who he ignores - braying like a donkey
in disclaiming feminine arts
like dancing in parks where whales sing)
had called me once upon a magpie's nest
to brew up troubles of her own.
On hearing how she'd destroyed herself -
and him (because one cannot play against the other
without tearing both to bits of heart and bone) ...
Rexine told me she'd lately risen
from the depths of hell, and was breaking
her heart to rejoin her masculine half.

Bed-ridden now, Rexine had once graced
stages of desire like Rex and I ...
or so it seems. I don't remember
now that Eileen, Rex's wife ...
or was it Pooch, or Pat, or Fatso?
That's it. Plumpy! They had a humpty-dumpty
time of it, too, it seems.
I left Rex as, speaking glow-words and dragon's teeth,
he sought to bind me to his will.
Eileen had glowed herself into other arms years ago.
She recently married the man she left Rex for.
He's only half her age ... how time flies
when you're in a stupor. Fancy fancying
anyone else when you're married to Rex.
Hang on. I was married to him myself -
or so it seemed in those desiring days
when the world was younger than a Ra spring -
or a Tiger's burning brightly
upon bottles shaped like female forms,
like those we drained when, dragging ourselves to death
and flaying ourselves alive,
we drove to parks where larks crowed
'which wine would monsieur' ... or was it 'madame?'
I forget because we always drank
whatever was offered, then stuffed
ourselves silly with chicken liver, fish, or WHALE MEAT!
sorry ... turtle soup. Once he took
Lucy and me dancing in to Williams,

treating us royally like the Romans we aren't
and he can't live up to - for while Lou Lou and I
pigged out on crayfish and crabs and mussels,
which helped build ours -
but not enough for me to biff him one in the eye
the night he tore strips off my uncritical flesh
after seeing Romeo and Juliet
when dancing in at the Hole, somewhat
the worse for wear now I'm no longer
bolstering them up in the daily press ...
Passion sits peevishly on Romans
whose songs call dreaming whales.
They tell me 'you're not wrong, Narelle,' ...
(an actress friend who plays her part
in this passionate passional)
'to reason rhymes and clown your way to hearts.'
In this word play, I get to lick my paws,
as Rex licked his after licking
platters clean of salt fry
in fry-ups greater than ours
when I upped and left him standing ...
no, I only let him sit
in a straight-backed chair - not lounge about
stroking his mane. That was the evening
after he'd played tennis
(which Rex plays better than me -
because I never get to play
the stuffing out of he who won't let me

play up now we've parted.)
Slinking into his chair, Rex
didn't like it a bit when, playing a game
of other's creation, I kissed his dirt-ridden paws.
Flooring myself in my purple suit
(that suits my purpose best
when I have to bless myself
and haven't a red cent to pay for it,)
I officiated - on Ra's command -
at the ceremonial return of Rex's female soul.
Learning Rexine had spent his aeons
in hells deeper than fire,
higher than kites can fly above the moon
and wider than a ghost's arms,
stretching winding sheets from unknown beds,
Rex grew grave, pondering how she could rise
so rapidly - considering her aeons in hell.
When Rexine visited me (prior to reunion with Rex,)
she begged we sit in the shade,
as being one herself she feared the sun.
The shade she called herself then was Rex -
for how was I to know his male and female selves
were severed? I might have been a shade myself
the day Rex took me for a ride in Kings Park.
The gloom I exuded, and the tears Ra rent
in relating that I was a new-christ-in-the-making!
In leonine days when lions prowled with tigers,
Amber cried ra ra ra ... no, Ra cried

hoorah for Rex, now he knows
the futility of ego since, smoothing my mane,
I gave him a poem called Giving It Up For Lent.
'Mew, very nice,' was all he could drag up.
But, speaking of giving things up,
Rex never disconnected Rexine at all -
she just severed herself with 'to-roo Silvio,
see you in a dragon's tear-drop,' no ...
'aeons later, in Rob's hell's kitchen.' Bye.

SONS AND DAUGHTERS OF DEATH

Doing the seven brides who wish me
well on the way to transportation's ice
a favour, I trade rings of fire
for cryptic creeds, finding myself borne
upon golden seas. On foreign shores,
I speak to crowds who drink my words,
draining dry their need to seek a sage.
Then, guiding my crew to lands
more distant, I sail again the dreaming stars,
beseeching Sirius to smooth the raging seas.
Trumpeting a clarion call, I summon hordes,
and clear the way to hearts by showing love.
Restored to peace, they please themselves -
thus pleasing Gaia. At life-tide's end
my soul drifts up, and sees
the green-clad earth below.
From blathering of hell, I rang the bell
on patriarchy, to manifest that peace
which passeth understanding.
By sharking up my loins, I played
the harmony which retunes hearts.
Believing isn't seeing, just as hearing

isn't knowing the truth. Only when I slide
beneath the belly of my whale, who, groaning
in its grief, delivers a new Christ,

Raw Gold

will I believe exactly what I see and hear.
Then my dreaming whale
may dive again to sound its depths.

BLUE HUMPED WHALES

Orange groves where children play, never hear
prophetic thunder. Leaves fall into a dust-bowl,
and raging storms drive children home,
causing swelling buds to sag upon the backs
of blue humped whales. Envisioning mountain goats
flung across a ditch in time, they see
new life dawning on a lake of lotus blossoms.
There, men and women break seals to live out
lives of peace, and recharged, see
an ancient fisherman glean a pearl
from out the muddy deep to set in Cyclops' eye.
Preying upon a mountain lion, Orion's Mars
tore to bits an unborn queen.
Only when he scatters forth her bones,
and claws his way to fame in common dress,
will I come safely home.
Spirit children, then full-grown, will own
the love which tore me limb from limb.

SUMMER PALACES

Golden beaches dreamt by whales
throw moving shadows across the stars.
Engendering freedom which creates new joy,
blue humped whales praise astral beings
for their dutiful intentions.
Treading high-summer roses to dust,
the human race carved swathes from golden slopes -
yet blackened lands rise green-clad.
Seeking summer palaces, delighted
astrals heap joy upon returning whales.

ANNUAL GENERAL MEETING OF WHALES

Words filter, like dust on a dry afternoon.
Apologies, reports, honoraria complete
we adjourn for other business
to the club where, sharking it up,
I queen my way to a king's heart
with promises of golden tarts.
Unskilled in culinary arts,
I burn them all to cinders.

BIRTH OF SUMMER WHALES

Waters of the moon, breaking silently,
slide new-born whales, which summon
their awakening strength to fight for Gaia.
Pink blossoms of youth rain petals
upon the backs of baby whales.
Nets of silver, trailing the rosy waters,
sieve salt fry from teeming lands.
They lie broken on beaches blackened
by ash. Joy comes to Gaia
when planetary dross is cleansed.

AWAITING BIRTH

Chosen by summer whales
swimming in seas of golden fire,
I cry misguided tears of joy.
Fearing uncharted islands
which rise to wreck my craft,
I let the sea carry me home.
Strewn with fragrant petals,
I await my birth.

BEACHED WHALES

Singing whales drive ancient fishermen
to rest on isles of frozen grief.
Tourists, basking on sands of gold,
lie waiting for sirens to sing
old songs of whales.

DOLPHINS AND WHALES

Dolphins and whales, who swim in seas
of burning fire, never say fie,
or fiddle a hot fandango,
concerning whys and wherefores.
Those sly old bastards bask
like hot potatoes in the sun,
burning my mind with questions -
yet riddle me with shit!

WHALES, AND OTHER HEAVY LUMBERERS

I'm a great heavy elephant, fantasising
one who thinks he knows me well,
yet never leaving well enough alone,
lumbers me with his disbelief in whales!
Lumbering along my way, I season
cakes, rapidly baked in brimstone fire,
and ale, chilled in hell's ice-room,
for the sole delight of queenly dolphins
and blue humped whales, who
keenly procreate their fat new calf.

DREAMING DONKEYS

Self-willed donkeys never wait
for winds to blow up storms of wrath,
they just play wearisome games,
hoping to keep problematic suns at bay.
Grazing in verdant pastures,
they pass away the days
churlishly calling kettles black,
while refusing to see
the pitch that tars their own pot.

SLINGING A SLANGER

Now isn't it funny, when I haven't any
money and Rex once offered me the world
that he fled when I said
Rexine - his soul-natured feminine self -
needed uniting with his heart,
so that waves of love could penetrate,
changing him from an intolerant,
egotistical dogmatist,
who insisted on assuming responsibility -
when, in my crapped-up confused hell,
he hadn't a cat's whisker's chance
of finding the thread for my SURVIVAL!

FREEDOM TO FIGHT

The rocket, having blown up in my face,
blew one who wills me best a long way off.
Having gone so far, he ordered I stand clear,
unload the locket I loved, and blow out my brains.
He then grew grave, declared war on the one
who knows him least, and events, transpiring evil,
blew us both apart. As a race, we who call ourselves
human, cannot compare with dogs - or,
for that matter, insects! Blindly, we grope
towards the sun, while devilishly daring the night.
Evil hearts, and crazy paper tigers,
ply their lotions to ulcerated parts
which never heal. Other potions, pouring balm
on troubled waters, brave the foolish virgins,
and fry new fish to please the one
who newly pleases herself. Rubbing remnants
of oil from platters licked clean by Jack and Jill,
I embraced the one who spoiled me the most,
and licked the last smear from his lips
before kissing him goodnight. Dreaming of battleships
that go bump in seas, and steal away keys
of conscious scheming, I drowned the one
who bumped me off my perch, climbed upon my place,
and groped his way to feed new fish.
Daring myself to face the one who lumped me
with the rest, left me high and dry,

and lifted himself up higher than he ought,
I fell upon my face and wished him well.
Dreamily I groped my way towards the hill of one
who, praising me the most, calls me pretty names
and plays heavenly games till late into the night.
Dragging myself from bed, I raced into the park,
meeting in the dark the one who brazens
out his breath, and bores me half to death -
but brings chocolates and artificial roses
to gladden my crazily beating heart.
Toasting the one who dries my tears the most,
drains my patience least, and queers himself
by roasting roots of glorious trees, I blame
myself for riding rivers of golden fish,
and, praising the one who loves and dares me most,
damns and tries me most, and adoringly parades
me most, I bless the day I died upon a grief,
rose upon a thorn, and laughed away my tears
to die upon a dream, rise upon a bud,
and close my eyes to one who, loving me the least,
squeezes me the most, and blesses himself not at all.
Saviours of sinners, and other felons,
praise the way I now let well enough alone,
and dry my dreams, never again to clamber
into beds unmade by one who tries my patience most,
pleases himself the least, and threatens war
whenever he fails to understand the one
who threw him out the door, blew his candle

out of hell-fire's reach, and traded old clothes
for new, to teach him how to love me now the best,
give his head a rest, and relieve his painful heart
by pinning mine to his chest. Loving him the best,
I drummed him out the door, dreamed him on the floor,
where visions never greet the one who damned herself
the most, called herself the host,
and drew her life to a willing close.
Seeming to dance her way to stars which praise
the ones who clapped her out of doors,
cried her not at all, and closed the bar again
to dry her dreams, she wonders how she stood there
in the dark, screaming like a lark in pain till,
slamming back the gate, she glimmered in the park,
and shoved aside the spark of anger in her heart
for one who praised her not at all,
and proved himself a straw-man, stuffed
with roaring paper tigers, who lay there in the dark,
waiting for the lark to sing returning songs of war.
Prizing myself the most, I call on hosts
who always love me now at least as much as he
who drives me up my tree, drawing me on to see
that Ra, Tiger Burning Bright and Sheer Khan
are the only three who love us equally.
Climbing down, I see the coast is clear of cats
who claw their paper tigers to death,
and clench their teeth of gold, to gleam
away the fire in one who paws her way to fame,

pools her love with those whose fearful sighs
fool her not at all, and knows they praise the day
their fevered brows were cooled between her amber paws.

GIVING IT UP FOR LENT

'Don't give me up,' he cried
upon a night-time strewn with grief.
Rex clutched me to his breast,
and rested his head on mine.
I praised him for the love he bore me,
deploring my own lack of passion.
Wondering why my arms grew slack,
he hacked me to death.
I rose again and took him back,
despite our changed relationship,
and gave him up for lent.
I have no regrets.
He, however, does not enjoy
his chastened state, and, lying alone,
lives only for others -
so cannot know the love he lacks himself.
Uneasy lies he who lives alone,
denying needs which keep him whole.
Finding Rex once more before my door,
I shut him in.
Decrepitude crept away,
and youth again brought hearts
which wept and prayed in silent grief together.
Praise be the little things in life.
Having raised each other up,
we live our lives alone.

She who lies alone lives for herself,
and others - as she chooses, and wins hearts
in ways she chooses, and sows seeds
in those she chooses, and loves
as only she may choose.
In choosing me, my lovers choose themselves
to be their own true loves.
In choosing themselves, my lovers choose me.
In giving it up for lent, I chose
the whale's way. Never again will I allow
any other ever to choose my way.
I choose ever to choose,
always to use my freedom of choice,
and never give others the power
to make choices which never were theirs.
In giving it up for lent, my passion,
now spent in daily loving myself more and more,
unfolds me like the budding rose,
to lose and find myself upon a thorn,
blown upon a grief, no longer torn
between an unknown ecstasy and former love.
Time heals the pricks and tears of past regrets
and eases present pain through joyous love.

LYING TONGUES

Rare western screeds, rolled in time's memory,
need no reading to foretell the gleam in Silvio's eye.
Aching in bone and flesh, he sighed
'I love thee, oh queen of my desire.'
My weakened heart needs a love to fill
its cavernous hell and vanquish all
but, believing in the mysterious passageways
which seal souls and give truths,
I unstoppered my basic line
and wept, 'thou lies in thy teeth.'

BLEATING THE LAMB

Narelle, who bleats the lamb to life,
evades her barking dogs of woe.
Climbing golden mountain slopes,
leaving the curs behind,
she flails through terrified friends
to grab the fins of dolphins,
frolicking in golden seas.
Hell's burning bells, escaping
like steam from sinking ships,
scream new-born pleasure
to testify against the tides of grief.
January the eighth when I'm reborn
unites the enemies of Calgary!

LOVES TRAFFIC IN THE DARK

When love was new, I played upon the stage of life,
and raised myself a little higher than the time
I played the part of angel in a play.
Now I grace the stage as goddess, and queen
of my desiring heart, I love as many as filled
the auditorium, in days I only played upon a stage.
Praying for the one who also graced that stage,
I hope to blow her candle of desire a little closer
to the one who loves her best - once more
to play angel on the stage of life.
Though parted now, Narelle and I have never
really been separate for an instant.
Playing angel again, she'll crew my craft,
which battles terrifying giants - like Cyclops
and Goliath - to drum up doves of peace,
which feed their fellow actors in starvation's face,
staring their eyes out, and merrily picking bones
which feed heavenly faces, and catch falling stars
to pace the limping days of wrath and reason,
straying on stages which war with roses
of a different odour. Hopefully, pleasure
will bring Narelle and me once more upon the stage
of parties who direct us to propose a new order
for the one who, bearing us best, allows us
to treat her worst of all. Trading my angel halo
for differently coloured clothes, I praise

her who blows me out the door to grace the one
who bears me daily on the stage of life.
Praising Gaia, I bless the day I died
upon a different cross. Desiring her welfare,
I rise early every morning and bear myself as one
who never lies beneath desiring trees,
which shed rose petals upon lovers in the park.
Praise be to Gaia who, dying to herself,
trades former glories - which we wasted -
for rivers of filth and salt-dredged lands.
Having no desire other than to see her once more
clear of kings who drain her dry, and queens
who bake their tarts from her living heart,
I know Narelle's not wrong when she returns
to parts as yet unknown, which savour those tarts
and, finding they stink to the highest heaven of all,
helps fling them in the eye of devils
who desire the heart of Gaia. Trading halos,
we bless the day we rose up early as larks
to sing the praise of kings and queens
who never bake tarts which stink to high heaven,
but battle their knights, (of an order
newly-awakened to the needs of their only mother, Gaia.)
Praise be to larks - and other creatures
who cleanse rivers of filthy water, by forcing
unsavoury knights to clean up their acts.
Heaven helps he and she who always help Gaia,
goddess and queen of all our hearts.

A RISEN NEW CHRIST

Mars, the living light, confers on me
his sword of truth, and flute of passion,
to play with all the keenness
of my mind and soul. Delivered
from beneath the belly of the whale,
I'll rise to fight the giant Cyclops,
and orchestrate a new world order
where newborn kings and queens
unyoke their ghosts of a chance, like Rex,
of ever winning spurious games of tennis,
racketeering away their days
in flinty-hearted, mindless ways
which cloud their souls.
Then heavenly hosts will praise the day
I offered up my will, raising spiritual children
to receive the sanctified rose.

RETURNED CHILDREN

Aligned by Jupiter with Mars
to battle demons of the one-eyed Cyclops
I commissioned a boat and rowed alone towards Gallipoli.
Summer whales, rising from the deep,
lashed gigantic tails against the stern.
Both oars lost
I lay down in the boat and drifted with the tide.
Flung out at night upon a narrow strip of beach
I woke to find Gallipoli's chiseled black glass cliffs.
A cry calls children home across the tides of grief,
and ancient cattle (spirit kin of this Hyperborean drive)
see Gallipoli's withered whore much changed.
To them this warring crone is Sarah, sweet mother,
but to me she's hag-moon Lilith, grandma in my alchemy
 of soul.
Glimpsing gold, she serenely awaits a sacrificial death.
Skipping over shores of an anguished, once divided land
the joy of children's ringing laughter will lay ghosts,
dissolve this lunatic Hyperborean curse
as freed souls raise heroes:
peace roses to expunge past woe.

CHAPTER 8

FRIENDS AND OTHER FELONS

Yesterday I spoke to a friend,
who is not so much a friend as a friendly felon.
Sam asked me over to share a meal recently
and as I rarely leave my hell's kitchen
(being still within the belly of the whale,)
I gladly accepted. On hearing about my host,
Sam thought to change my name to Joan,
Jonah's sister. Having spent a mere three days
in his whale's belly, Jonah was vomited
on a beach, and made to bless himself -
and others - who, doubtless, were
as distrustful of God as he.
Not that I know my Bible stories well -
but I'm getting to know them better
since entering this whale's belly!
I've been here four months now,
and when another three have passed
I'll be reborn, then slide beneath
this dreaming whale to where I've yet to know.
But having no regrets, I'll do what's needed,
and go with the one called Bob to India, China, Japan.
anywhere at all he wants to go.
But that's another chapter and verse in my book.
I'm visiting Lucy today -
which concerns my host, for he likes friends
to visit me - which pleases me

as now I'm seeing more people
than when I worked all day at the A.B.C.
then all night at theatres
where I criticised or not - as the case may be -
which proves my point that all felons
practising the art of wordly ways
should remember that actors are human, too.
Rex never let me forget
that I was once a critic, and it cost us
many tears - especially when we saw
Romeo and Juliet who, according to Rex
did none too well. I keenly considered the show
and thought … not that it matters now -
but Rex never let it alone.
He picked and clawed his bones near half to death
and, after splitting hairs about the play, we split.
But it was time we parted.
Rex had barked me up a tree
by monkeying with my heart for much too long -
but that's a former chapter and verse.
And now that he has cleared out,
taking away his bones - and bottle
of Eau De Cologne from my bathroom cabinet,
(but left a Johnny Walker lurking in my kitchen cupboard).
Yes, now I think on, it was Rex who walked out,
leaving her who walked out on a husband and daughter,
people who nowadays seem like ghosts
because they haunt me a bit …

but getting back to Rex -
please don't think he took away anything
he, himself, hadn't placed in my cupboards ...
like the silver - which I haven't got
and he only threatened to steal,
whenever he dealt me one in the eye
for not being able to sleep with him by my side.
Rex only took items he'd left
in earlier happier days ... apart from a packet
of Quick-Ease - he forgot to take that.
Rex needed them, he said
to relieve his heartburn -
never allowing me to relieve it for him,
(or his addiction to cigarettes - a habit
Rex is trying to kick,) which was stupid
as I'm brilliant at busting addictions!
In Touch For Health, (an alternative mode
that my host predicts will for me
soon be out of date) we fix not only addictions,
but phobias, obsessions, fixations -
and a whole heap of structural, emotional
and nutritional things. I once cured Jill
of her addiction to cigarettes and she loved me for it.
She, too, now is a friendly felon,
for flinging herself from me,
it seems she's decided a goblin holds me enthralled.
Jill goes by many names from lifetimes past.
Cassandra, she who prophesied in former days,

told me that as Jezebel, Jill was a lecherous,
lascivious ... but no - mustn't contravene
professional ethics revealing private karma.
Prophets like Cassandra weren't welcome
in days of yore - and no more are they now,
for blue horses, daily urging riders towards the sun,
shun those who climb trees of gold
to peer into the future.
In so doing, they never please anyone.
And it doesn't please me to be kept here
dreaming up trees at four in the morning
while my host bashes my ear-drums.
Returning to that meal with Sam -
his cuisine was superb! We began with almond soup,
then had vegetarian lasagne, followed by
pears topped with yoghurt and coconut -
a feast for a queen! And how I queened it ...
or did Sheer Khan? Yes, that purring, clawing cat
really queened it, no, socked it to him
later that night when I banged his back and front ...
No, it was Sheer Khan who banged his front and back,
transferring, so she called it,'certain energies'
in an alarmingly violent hug!
He must have needed extraordinary power,
because usually when she bangs 'em,
they're more or less ready - being concerned
more with spiritual matters than power.
Sam's into power these days like one possessed.

That's why Sheer Khan (and the other two)
had to bang him so soundly.
In sounding him out in the past,
they found he was up to things
they try to erase - like making more money
than we actually need. Sam's learned heaps
about manifestation since scourging himself
in Margaret River. Impoverished,
and traumatised by love, he read books
to please himself - and Caesar!
Now with power to manifest his dreams,
Sam should know that money's not the end
but just the means. Time to go.
Toodle-pip. It's up with the lark to crow about a bit.
Wait. I've been up with the raven,
ravening on about larks and crows -
so I'm not about to go on stages
other than those where angels sing.
See you when I've caught an hour by the wing
and dreamed myself to blissful parks.
God bless, and may you all have blissful dreams.

THE WHITE BALLOON (MARK 1)

'Jesus is coming this Christmas.
I asked him to call and he sent me a sign:
a beetle, clearly marked with a cross,
walked in through my door this morning,'
said Susan, Sam's wife.
It was a lovely Christmas.
We lit sparklers, squeaked squeakers,
blew whistles, put on paper hats,
drank and feasted, growing mellow
in each other's company.
We were less our separate selves,
more than our numbers' sum.
A white balloon drifted to the ceiling
above our hostess's head. 'You see?
Jesus said he would come,' she said.

THE WHITE BALLOON (MARK 2)

'Jesus is coming this Christmas.
I asked him to call and he sent me a sign:
a dung beetle, clearly marked with a cross,
walked in through my door this morning,'
said Susan, Sam's wife.
It was a beautiful Christmas.
We lit sparklers, squeaked squeakers,
blew whistles, put on papers hats,
drank and feasted, growing mellow
in each other's company.
When Jesus rose to the ceiling
in the shape of a white balloon,
he soon found himself floored by all the dung,
which the beetle had collected,
rolled up in a ball, and thrown at Lazarus,
who, rising upon a thorn,
biffed us one in the eye for getting him up
when he was resting his head,
and only playing at being dead.

CHRYSALIS

Harrowed by hate, his departed harpy wife
still shrieking in his ears, furrowed
by lost, past, ever-present love,
gorged gut-full, a man pupates.
Cocooned against the world,
the country farm house gives its balm.
From ancient gums' cathedral, magpies
carol benediction. A shepherd barks commands
to his dog. Heard distantly
sheep bleat, and cattle ruminate
as wind sighs through pines outside the home.
Fire crackles, and a kettle sings
upon the hob. Meditating metamorphosis,
the man awaits time to soften pain.
Redefined, his strength rewon, he bursts
a shell of calcified un-nameable terror,
rising on dazzling wings to meet the sun.

DESERT SANDS

The making of millions of pieces of gold
weighed heavily on one who stayed up later
than he ought. Grasping for a fate
worse than life, he desired wealth
which signalled across seas of burning sand.
Deserted by three wives, he stood alone,
shading his eyes from the glare,
then sallied forth, his robes
winding their way to his knees.
Glittering gold lay all around.
He packed his saddle bags and rode off home.
Triumphantly he bore the booty up,
sure his dream was won. Seeing wholly gold,
he poured out sand.

HUNGER OF MY HEART (MARK 1)

'Hunger of my heart,' Rex said, and the chasm
of a private hell yawned deep. What was I,
standing framed between kitchen and a laundry doorway,
that Christmas Eve we met? Later, over fish,
eyes distant, 'I remember you,' he said.
Seeing archetypes, he called me his 'butless lover,'
I was a vision in yellow, and my golden hair
crowned mother, mistress, goddess, queen.
Human now, I am 'Anglo-Saxon' - drab, deficient,
sexually plain: a disappointment in his Latin eyes.
But still he clung - shoring me against
wolves and satyrs that prowled and grinned.
Orphaned, he told me of an aunt who promised:
'if you're good, I'll love you …'
I hold him tight, willing my tears to wash away
hidden, ancient fears, and my heart,
in a rush of love, obliterate his hell.

HUNGER OF MY HEART (MARK2)

'Hunger of my heart,' Rex said, and the chasm
of a private hell yawned deep. What was I,
standing framed between kitchen and laundry doorway,
that Christmas Eve we met? Later over fish,
eyes distant, 'I remember you,' he said.
His archetypes of goddess, queen, mistress, mother,
and other female lovers of dreaming whales,
blocked my mind when I was his vision in gold.
I'd drawn him back, it seems, to earlier times when,
unbidden, he had waited in parklands among
a flock of blue horses. Now 'Anglo-Saxon,'
(a breed seedier than his fearless Romans,)
I'm drab, deficient in his eyes - yet still
he shores me against wolves and satyrs,
prowling and grinning from behind the masks
of forlorn angels. Now, having no regrets,
I won't be taken for a fool, who, unlike my mother,
cannot delve into ways phoney and porny ... Polony!
What I mean is, unlike a former lover
of blue dreaming whales, who never regrets
having no regrets ... and having no regrets
I do not like it when my mother does not get nuts
and chocolates, like the box Rex once gave Jean.
He gave her only trouble, by masquerading
as a saintly dragon, and drawing out his breath
in friendly sighs. Mistaking spirit gold,

he said I was 'schizoid,' never seeing my truth
amid the maze of lies.

COMET ROCK

Time raced. Events spread evenly
against the wall. Bill Haley's band,
playing fifty's rock, laced lunch
with prophesies of rage, to erupt
volcanic, cataclysmic change.
Only my father's wrath,
and my sister's stubborn pride
matched my desire to know
creation's secret which, bursting
from a star, judges the axiom of my fall.
Time races. Creation's organism,
where summer dries the land to dust.
A fierce sun woos the lotus,
and sends her petals flying in the breeze
to open time's thousand-eyed wraith,
and speculate upon the rose
of gross and glorious gods.
Time race. Unevenly matched,
I never questioned roads which led the Roman
to my door, or I to his.
I only know my path twists around
the sacred rose.

CHAPTER 9

HAVING NO REGRETS

Having no regrets, I waited upon a tow truck
which eventually sprang up, just as Ra promised.
'In bad old days, when knights rode chargers,
they never waited to be told their clutch cables
were anything less then sound,' he said.
'How the hell,' I asked, 'can that help me
now Bugsy's busted her clutch, and wasted my time
in this park? How can I call on Gyula
if, may hap, he happens to phone?
And having left home without my notebook,
how can I scribe your words, unless I use
the back of this shopping list to satisfy
your slavedriver's whip-cracking pace?'
And now, as I'm waiting for the tow truck
to truck Bugsy away to the garage,
I hope I won't be late to have my hair cut,
as the one called Matthew's coming around
to see me soon. I met Matthew at a place
called Home Base, where Gyula
had asked me to spell him when he went for a drink.
He was massaging necks and backs ...
or was it shoulders and knees?
Not that it matters much, as all he wanted me to do
was do my best for his clients
by giving them a good rub around the neck
or balance their fourteen muscles.

And what a cockle up Ra made of that
when he caused me to emit howls and shrieks
that were frightening enough to freak a ghost!
The clients, however, felt much relieved
by my manner of work, so I didn't much mind
being made to act the howling healer.
And judging by crowds that gathered
to watch me work, I became Home Base's
star attraction - not that it helped at all
to build up my clientele. I suppose
people felt it safe to see me in a place
I couldn't eat 'em - despite
my chucking myself at 'em, as if Ra
meant to gobble them heart and soul.
Matthew asked me to fix up his back,
which was giving him hell. On tuning in,
Ra said Matthew was my Simon called Peter,
and that I must work with him free of charge.
So I blew his back apart to make it whole
and healthy, and he told me later that a friend
in the business of psychic healing had seen
great waves of energy leave his back.
The man who trucks away intractable cars
like Bugsy, has just lifted her up
on the back of his truck. He told me
some car owners don't like to see
their dream machines hooked up behind
to be hauled unceremoniously away -

that's why he invented a way of winching them up,
so they could ride to a garage
in dignity befitting their style.
Now Bugsy's safe and sound inside this garage,
I can walk across the road to have my hair cut.
I'm glad I'm no Samson - although once I thought
being shorn of my crowning glory
would necessarily sheer my power
to attract the adulation of lovers
of long golden hair. Twice I've grown it
to a length past my waist which drew
long loving looks. So Gordon
was just a bit miffed when, following the honeymoon,
I had it shorn like a sheep, for as we'd be
camping in Europe, I didn't want the nuisance
of untangling a long mane of hair.
Before inextricably tangling my life with Gordon's
I had a year of knowing the bliss
of choosing to go and come as I please.
I was living in Melbourne, and found in Keith
(who changed his name to Michael, finding
that it gave greater substance when seeking
work as an actor) a friendship as rich
and rewarding as it was rare.
As two disgustingly healthy, naively zestful
lovers of life, we shone like beacons at Tats,
that scungy, dingy pub which, patronised by the push,
made creative singularity the norm.

We met actors, musicians, philosophers,
and a whole bunch of highly laudable
but often quite dubious folk, who initiated us
into a cruel, though colourful life.
Keith's friendship made my time in Melbourne
as happy as the carefree years of childhood,
when Alice showed me selfless love.
Wherever I wanted to swim was always okay with her,
and she knew where the best fishing
and picnic spots were. Alice was the only one
to whom I could express all the stumbling,
desire-filled ramblings of inarticulate youth.
Rambling from the serenity of a love so
undemanding,
I'll rumble my preference for passivity
by relating how Rex demanded
I be exactly what he thought I ought,
and never allowed me to be what I was -
a highly unsophisticated and easily pleased
complex, volatile, argumentative woman
who will not let sophisticates like Rex -
who are never easily pleased - dictate her opinions.
Rex never accepted my loving him simply,
when love that's simple is all I've got to give.
He venerated power as force to move the universe,
never perceiving that love's the only means
by which the universe moves. At times, though,
love's an ashen rose. Rachael refuses to see me

until after settlement, and I long for the time
when we can be together, without the hurt
of my having left home rankling her heart.
Not long after leaving home, I phoned Rachael
asking her to ask her father to visit a doctor
concerning his heart. I'd been receiving
distress signals through auric energy wires,
and knowing he'd never accept my Touch for Health,
had asked his heart what healing it would like,
and it chose visiting a doctor.
However, on relating this request to Rachael,
she slammed down the phone. I waited
some minutes, then rang her again -
to be tearfully told that Touch for Health
would never ever ever by allowed
to touch their hearts again!
So now that the number of hearts
which have slammed their atrioventricular valves
in my greenly irradiating spiral of fire
has narrowed the field, I'm still yearning
for Bob McCloud to brighten my day with a call,
saying how wrong he was to bawl me out
and allow a true-hearted soul to grieve -
that'd really lighten my load,
and buck up my spirits. However,
I'll just have to endure this riderless blue horse,
and rack off. So to-roo all you lovely folk
who are free to party, and play away your days.

Perhaps one day I'll see you in a dog's starry eye.
Sirius soon ... Sirius - the star
which glimmers in the dolphins' eye. Bye.

THE MAD JACK-UPPER OF ROSE TREES

Juliet said as she lay down in bed
'pray heaven I have no disease,
for somehow I know from the tip of my toe
to my head, I am not really free.'
Her brother, called Jack, got up
at the crack of dawn, and declared he would see
if somehow or other a good little brother
could just have a look at her knee -
and other items of interest to a hot-blooded Latin,
it may help her appreciate
that being free was not as bad
as people like Diamond and Lil try to make out -
however, if she'd rather be incarcerated,
he'd be happy to lock her up in arms
which would never let her enter the woods
of desiring whales, and then if it ailed her
to be upbraided by one who thinks she has to please him
by being the wife, mother and goddess
of his desiring, he'd be happy to provide
the one person in the world to rid her
of the need to fill those misery-laden shoes.
Juliet fell to her knees, kissed Jack's shoes,
then threw herself into her brother's lap,
parting his hair with her grief-stricken sighs.
'Pray, little brother,' she said, 'how am I
to fill my misery-laden shoes, when others

please to take them dancing? How am I
to find shoes to fit my prince, when I have none
befitting me?' Jack replied with a corny grin,
'please yourself. I only hoped to assist
you gain entrance to the woodland ball,
being held tonight in the ancient hall
behind the shed.' Juliet pleased herself,
and taking her brother's hand, strolled
nonchalantly with him into the woods.
When sacred rites had been prepared, Juliet
lay upon a patch of clover to relieve
her diseased mind of its longing to be free.
Believing her freedom went windward to one
who never should have taken it, Juliet
pleased herself again and again and again.
The pair, strolling none too nonchalantly home,
prepared to die once more that night -
telling lies concerning their whereabouts
to folk who felt they needed to know.
When night came, however, Juliet
fell pregnantly silent. Desiring her brother dead,
she fell upon him lustfully and broke his neck.
Jack upped and, taking his head in his hands,
begged his sister to mend the broken part.
Having no remorse, Juliet exclaimed 'never,
never again will I place my secret heart
in your filthy hands to lose in woods where roses
spill their perfume on the terminally ill.'

Jack, bleeding profusely from the neck,
disdained his sister who rejected his pleas
for assistance when he needed her most,
and mended the broken part himself.
Perfectly patched, Jack discovered he could
similarly heal his sister. Freely dispensing
his heart, he took her back to the woods
and redefined the art of making love.
Only when he discovered the art of healing
could Jack truly mend his sister's desire to be free.
Then once more he loved his Juliet, who he found
was not his sister at all - because Juliet's parents
adopted Jack when his parents died.
Declaring themselves free,
the happy couple lived and loved forever after.
Praising God, they grew old and young together,
and finally died upon a rose bush, propagated
from one in the woods, where they'd lain
so long ago. Juliet's heart lay buried
beneath thorn trees, because she'd killed
her lover. Jack's lay buried with Juliet's,
and together the two hearts grew as one
into a crowned rose. Peace roses, palely pink,
shed their petals upon snow which covered
grave stones, linking hearts which never die,
but only fade away in roses. However,
it cannot be said as I fall into beds of snow,
that I will ever leap up dead and cry

Raw Gold

'hail the new king.' As yet within the whale's belly
I can only say 'snow the new rose,'
and know that what I really mean is
'long live the queen who breaks necks
to learn that love is never what it seems.'
Aiming to please others, I fail to please myself.
Aiming to please myself, I please others anyway.
However, as it pleases others, I please myself
to love the one who loves me back in desiring woods
which whales love most. Now that I'm
well and truly dead, I long once more
to be loved by my Jack, under trees
which love us both backwards in time.
Jack and I live happily between lives
as brother and sister, because in fact
we are all brothers and sisters
in the soul of one who cries us all to death.
Upbraiding myself daily, I grow petals
to strew on new lovers who venture in these woods
to die in each other's arms. Charming couples -
I believe I see one before me now.
Why it's Jack and me - together
at last night's ball in the ancient woodland hall.
Weren't we wonderful the way we
locked ourselves together for life?

PRESENTS FROM HELL

Straying over pages of a diary,
I ceased living in the past and future,
died, and rose instantly, knowing
living only in the moment to be worthwhile.
Then I saw that what was written was not a diary,
but my life. Not knowing what to think
concerning words which I, myself, had written
when young, I cried out plaintively for help.
A voice replied, 'don't look back,
never look back, do not ever again look back
to see the life you left behind.'
Now I look ahead. I only see what lies in front.
I never return to places which broke my heart.
Now I go to places where my heart stays whole.
Now I travel paths which please me.
Now I only go where I am welcome.
Now I know that formerly - when I drew a blank
at many doors - I rang the bell
of my own desiring heart. Now when I ring bells,
I do so with a wholesome heart, and receiving
messages of love, daily eat my bread with joy.
Now I freely enter doors marked 'entrance,'
that formerly were closed. Presents from hell,
delivered to my door, bring even greater joy
than those received when life
was younger than a tiger's spring,

sweeter than the rose of peace,
braver than the icy wind that seared my face
and brought me peace of mind.
I know now that my former troubles
stemmed from insufficiently loving myself,
and not telling he I loved the most
just how very unhappy I was -
not with him, but me. So now I must tell him
that he may learn to love himself anew.
Praising the Lord's way, I brave new hearts,
finding them not yet home. However, I will never
train my finger on beams or bells to tell
my lovers I have called to cry my eyes out
over spilled joy of former loves. Praise be
to bellows from hell that blew away my will,
so I may rise to seek myself anew, and, finding
new truth, rise upon a dream to cry
'I love thee,' to myself again.

HEALTH: A PRESENT FROM HELL

I need never concern myself about my health again,
nor need I feel concern for those I love,
because my healing hands will never whoosh
and shove where they're not wanted.
I needn't feel concern about acquaintances,
because no one will ever complain
I acted incorrectly. Believing is not seeing,
just as hearing is not having faith
in one who loves me most of all.
Now I need not fear to question,
knowing that paradoxical answers contain the truth.
Training my ear to hear, is not just a matter
of clearing the dust of former years,
it necessitates an obedient heart, and keen eye,
to know and see that what I'm told
is not a pack of lies. Now that I'm well grown
within the belly of the whale, I know
that I, myself, must never tell lies -
unless I mean to deliver presents
from another kind of hell.

HAPPINESS ALWAYS BEGINS AT HOME

Happiness, unlike sadness, always begins
by crossing tees and dotting ies with axes
which cut trees, and oxen which draw ploughs.
Hearts which do not allow for oxen, axes -
or any privately-owned abandonment
of an ancient and more orderly order,
leave us none the wiser, and a lot worse off
than members of a crass and careless order,
who impose implements of vice - like tyrants,
who love those stoic souls which choose
never to grow easier than a tiger's spring,
or younger than a thorn in the side of the only king -
which caused his kingdom to topple.
Simple pleasures, like seeing how serenely
berries hang on their trees, lark song
and the chirruping of linnets, draw birds of prey
to pray for peace - and lions
to dam up eyes, and stopper hearts,
hounding mistresses who walk inappropriate paths.
Desiring these simple joys through Christ's path
recreates God's kingdom.

HAIR

Golden glory!
Let down those shining tresses
and mount your dreams.
Snip.
Samson crumbles,
Godiva falls.
Hair in a bottom drawer.

ALICE

Comfort, love's chief component,
came to me mainly from Alice.
She alone was love,
never criticising,
or attempting to judge.

CONCRETE JUNGLES, AND OTHER PARKLANDS

I loved my lover when he loved me,
the night I held his hand, and called him
my new love. 'I never knew how much you cared,'
he said. I never knew I cared whether
he lived or died. However, now I know my mind
a little better than when I nightly died
to the one who called me wife, I never care
these days whether I live or die, because now
it doesn't seem to matter two hoots
whether I live or die to others,
or to just myself.

CHAPTER 10

PLEASANT WALKS IN THE BLUE PARK

When younger than a tiger's spring
and sharper than a paper tiger, barking up trees
to please myself, I drew the dragon of desire
and married one who filled my life with joy.
Another dragon, drawn from out the deep,
then drew his fiery sword and slew my ease.
Time heals pain, they say, bringing pleasures new.
Though few and far between, I take mine now
in little things: a purple daisy, growing
by the path, a heron, dainty and serene,
dipping its beak to fish the river. And Gyula
rang me up today, desiring that I visit -
but as my car's in dock, Ra must take me on his back
if I'm to call. Striking up his band of furry cats,
(who nip and claw me on these days to draw my ire
and fire my future) Ra desired I phone the garage,
and collect my car. He hates the places
storing fumes which poison Gaia, longing
for better days, when electricity powers cars.
I, too, desire a time when current modes of travel
change, and we are free from toxic gas, which,
as Ra says, stinks to the highest heaven.
Bugsy - that's what I call my dream machine
whenever she fouls me up, for breaking hearts
and clutches, she drives me wild! Betsy,
(or rather Elizabeth, a name I learned

just now means loving God to death,)
is what she's named when, purring along nicely,
I'm deceived into believing she's a reliable car.
And now for a cup of bai lin tea to drive
me on my day. The god Bai Lin - like Ra
and his bunch of cats - rarely
lets me sleep these days - or nights. No go.
I just can't seem to wake up to myself -
or anyone else. Perhaps a coffee
will help … Ah, better. And I've had a little sleep -
in which I learned a good deal more
about the god Bai Lin. An ancient,
very venerable Chinese, he pleases souls
who tease out threads from hearts. He told me now
it's not just Ra who roars me on, for Bob,
the male in me, daily goads my soul.
Desiring to know my future, I asked
Bai Lin what lay in store. He said that
though now hanging from a winter thorn,
my life glowed summer on a distant moon.
And seen just now in a waking dream,
secret houses, arching their peaks towards the sky,
tempt me in where, borne upon the backs
of singing whales, I harmonise a golden theme.
Remembering the night that I lay steaming
in a bath at Bob's - a little smaller than I like,
but large enough for two (or was it six,
who pleased us when they pleased themselves?)

I long for summer to erase my silent tune.
One sacred love now fills my heart,
and binds it tight. Craving arms the night
I lay upon a cold, yet desire-filled table,
I gave my love to one who craved my praise.
Placing gemstones at strategic points
along my body, Bob balanced me with crystals.
They worked their magic, while he worked his.
Pleased with results, he asked
if there was anything else that I required.
I asked him for a hug - which he gladly gave
before changing places with me on the table
so I could balance him. Circling wildly,
the pendulum swung about his rings of fire and ice
then, requesting I pendulate a second time,
he was mortified when the crystal hung quite still.
Bob admitted then, to training the first one
with his mind - so making me think his chakras
were fine. In the morning, when we rose
from sleep, I used a method of my own
to gauge his health - and found
that his emotional energy was nil. No wonder
the pendulum had drooped! Knowing his cup
was empty, he disdained to fill up mine,
for after breakfast (which I ate alone -
as in the morning, he disdained food, too)
Bob submitted to a balance using Touch for Health,
but disliked my interference, preferring always

in matters of health, to go it alone.
He did say, though, that it was time he
'came in from the cold,' by which
I took it he meant he needed a special friend -
which especially pleased me. Our parting
later that day had been very friendly -
so when next week at Tafe, following
an Anatomy and Physiology lecture, he summonsed
me brusquely with 'now you,' it somehow sounded
friendship's doom. Shivering in the cold night air
beside my car, Bob told me then not to expect him
for dinner that Saturday night. And not just that,
he said he'd never allow me to love him -
suggesting, though, I love the little boy in me
called Bob. Concerning his change of heart,
he said he'd rather kick my teeth in now,
than break my body - later. Such violence
coming from him was a shock.
I believed him to be an altruist - but then,
we all can make mistakes. Bob always
kicked my teeth in when I rang. Once, desperate
for a friendly word from him I phoned because
gorilla, white owl, snake ... and a host
of tyrannic tigers and clawing cats
were giving me hell. Bob refused, however,
to let me speak - so snake hissed in his ear.
Snake told me later he'd scented something
cynical about Bob, and desired to satisfy himself

that he was sound. So following Ra's advice,
(and a visit to Salina - she who lives
in a Freo spirit house filled with beautiful things,
and who gave me holy stones stuffed with messages
to decode) I called on Bob one Saturday afternoon,
finding him in the garden - but not at home to me.
Concerning a matter of particular interest -
migrating souls - Ra had ordered me out
to learn from Bob if he knew his soul
often resided with me. Mine frequently
transmigrates to him - or so it seems,
for without clairvoyance, I can't yet see
whether souls themselves migrate - or send
their energy. I'd wanted to ask Bob
if he felt his soul's absence - it being
then with me. He, however, felt only the need
to rid himself of me, for scraping the dirt
off his fingers, while carefully avoiding
my eyes ... Ra had previously bidden
my close attention to this, saying
that unless Bob looked me in the eye, he lied!
Mumbling matters about which he could only guess,
Bob pontificated that, as my father
seemed somewhat remote, the male in me
lacked substance - suggesting that I take
a good long look at myself, and squint rejection
squarely in the eye! That was when Ra stepped in,
violently shaking me up. Leaving without so much

as a cup of rosehip tea to tease hospitality's muse
I crossed myself off the slightest possibility
of seeing Bob again. But Ra had different ideas.
Once he's dug his claws in, he's loathe to let go!
To ease my chagrined heart that night,
I listed names - as Bob desired - of those
I thought had caused rejection. But writing down
father, mother, sister, husband, daughter …
and everyone else in my life who seemed
to offer a hurt, incensed me. Calming my fury,
Ra advised I tear it up, and never ever negate
myself like that again! He sees rejection
as mirroring our faults, and says it's vital
to heal our aching hearts through self-responsibility!
But now Bob's finally barked me up a gum tree,
and ring-barked my heart, I need every scrap
of healing I can get. Well, toodle-pip.
See you when a helping heart calls round.
Don't ring-bark hearts you love, now, will you? Bye.

PLEASING THE MANY BY PLEASING THE FEW

Pleasing those who love to please themselves,
I wait upon pleasure to place raw gold -
the soul light of coming new Christs -
where make-shift treasure sinks. Thinking
of the way that berries hang coolly
and serenely upon boughs, I await my host
to change the hearts of those who traffic stones
as the only currency they know.
A new and taller order, waiting impatient
in the wings, bears witness to the way
that real treasure - our heads and hearts -
tune up, soon to sing their mysteries.

RADIANT WATER

Pleasure measures itself in seed sown.
Joy, barking its shins on pleasure's heels,
reaches zones where passion radiates to unknown seas.

CETATION DREAMS

Goaded by gods to send mercurial visions
to one much loved, I oil my face.
Dreaming of fish bearing golden icons,
I wake in ecstasy.

VISIONS SEEN IN A CUP OF TEA

Stupefied from sleep, I wake
to jangling bells, and take
dreams' tokens to the top-most deck.
Terrified passengers, on board
the ship Bai Lin, fearing fires from hell
raging up seas of wrath, clamber up
to drink their steaming cups of oolong tea.
Trading posts in ports along the way
send out small boats to parade their wares
of gothic skulls. Damming up my dreaming mind,
I envision an ancient yellow rose,
whose withered petals cling to life.
Beside it, a budding crimson rose
bursts brilliantly open.

I MUST HAVE FAITH IN THE PROCESS OF MY REBIRTH

Stand up and fight, you lily-livered bastard!
Ra, Tiger Burning Bright and Sheer Khan
command you brighten up and show some spirit.
Come round to the place near the zoo in South Perth
where crazy animals are housed and let's talk shop.

PLAYING A WAITING GAME

Brazening out my days within the belly
of the whale, I wait upon his will
to know my mission. Longing to lie again
in arms, mine only for a night,
I strum the lute of grief,
praying for one whose wrath for me
equals rage he bore the mother
who languished in his arms.
Playing a waiting game, I may not tell
my love to any other, until once more
I lie beneath his breast,
and feel his head on mine.

APPLE BLOSSOM PAIRS

Life, which rising from the grave
to bear the soul anew, preys on former days
when, stealing away upon crosses of a different order,
it lives to lie again in graves. Famished hearts,
rising to drink of the life which never dies,
please God. Those who fabricate lives,
draw conclusions which ruminate upon themselves.
Others, who many times lose and find their way
upon the path, one day will memorise
a waiting game, and play it well.
Only waiting's indolence allows memories
of losing and winning at life to balance out
the grief of ages. Passion leaves by an inner gate,
and at the door marked 'exit,' truth flies in.
Both youth and age dive deep to bring up pearls
from within the mouths of babes. Treasure, lying
within easy reach, flies up to strike the eye,
and draws us on to brighter days
where non-existent time makes meaningless the way.
Pleasure plays unevenly upon hearts
which please themselves. Pain, which passes
even unto death, plays little part
in those that grieve, and lie in beds of woe.
Pleasure and pain, arising from the need to be,
pass unevenly away, and play no part in lives
that fish for treasure in their deeps.

Daughters of death, having little desire
to please themselves, please others by diving
for pearls which have a different glow.
Rowers upon the river of life fish suns from skies,
where early worms catch birds of prey,
and rise to wriggle in nets of gold.
Prizes glittering beyond the skies, drive
chariots to discover hope in sullen smiles,
and grief, riven in misery, prepares a death.
Parading two by two, couples go their separate ways,
living lives which lubricate the flesh,
but dry the soul. Apple blossom pairs,
who greet each day anew, and share
their grief and pleasure, bless the day
they lived to praise themselves.

LOVE SONG TO MYSELF AND A SINGING WHALE

Sharking days and dreary plays
grow skinny in the waist. To bear my bust
I firmly must never let lust overwhelm me in baths
arriving hotter and later than spring.
Men and women who build bridges of trust
but never cross them in summer, as homewards
they wend ways to sharpen lores,
and clean out drawers of gold dust -
never own hearts drumming dreams which scheme
their way to passion's flower. Nowadays,
I never hope for baths from hell's kitchen
to fling shark-fin soup about, like largess
from the daughters of a tribe of kings.
Blowing kisses in the park, I desire
to catch a fin or two, and scuttle
across seas of fire and ice to claw my way
on crusts of bread, threading needles of ice,
and scraping Beethoven's fiddle to riddle-me-ree,
waiting to see the irony contained in trees
which never shed leaves of gold, yet invariably
bare busts, and lust after fire.
Blackened by night, I clambered into bed
beside the one who, weakened by desiring daughters
of foundationless kings, bid me flavour
my shark-fin soup with a little salt

from the seas of passion. Grinding gold to dust,
I sometimes dream of him who, desiring to bend
my mind to his own, merely strengthened my will
to bind myself to a whale. Now, winding my way
among stars, fiery with visions of new queens,
I glisten in the dark, sparking up a host
who rows me to where I'm loved the most.
Believing I have sinned more than my share,
I roar away ghosts who, drumming my dreams,
reveal fate's lucky dip. Pulling out a plum,
I stay longer in fabulous parks, where
glowing in the dark to dream my dreams
and think my thoughts and ride my rivers of fire,
I endlessly wait, till sliding from beneath
the belly of a fish, golden as summers without end,
I finally wend my way to one who seeks me
beneath a dream, ironic and wry, to dry me
in the sun forever in my face. A thousand suns
now beam upon the place where, stewing
in the whale's belly, I race away my time,
rhyming unseasonable reasons, to follow
where no footsteps ever go.

CHAPTER 11

ROSE-COLOURED FACETS

When soundly sleeping in my bed, the whale
biffed me one in the head. I shuddered and died,
then leapt up and cried 'ole, ole, ole -
I lie, I lie, I lie in saying I'm okay
without him who lies me down nightly
and rightly loves me to death.'
A tiny blister on my leg bubbled, bellowing
that what I need to make life light-hearted is love,
for without it this blister may swell to explode
the fallacy that I can live quite happily alone.
When making a cup of oolong tea just now,
my lionish kittens commanded I cut out pictures
of a mother and child which were on the packet.
They wanted me to put them with birthday
and other celebratory cards I've been saving,
to give to hospitalised children.
'Good one, Robsie,' I thought as it summoned a tear.
Ra's winking approval and invitation to treat myself
with my own chocolate biscuits
entreats I love myself for the idea -
(and being manifest in my flesh,
he's likely to love only polishing off the biscuits!)
Recalling having polished fleshy manifestations myself
as masseuse at a West Perth clinic,
I remembered a particularly modest youth named James,
who requested I pay considerable attention

to his back, having problems with a vertebrae.
He wouldn't allow me to work below
what he considered the line of decency -
seeming to stretch his swimming trunks
from neck to knee. Then, when I left the clinic
and was working at home, Ra decreed
I heal the light of his misaligned spine,
ordering I direct energies to specific spots
next time he came for a massage.
Having forgotten Ra's suggestion I conserve my strength,
I went into town (also at Ra's request) to outfit myself
for a job he'd promised I'd win in crown law.
So when James came I was tuckered out,
having traipsed endlessly round Myers' new store.
But I set to, giving the massage with heart, sending light
to the multitudinous deviations in James' spine -
which vibrated me violently throughout the whole process.
Depleted, I lay down afterwards to rest, requesting
he stay on the massage table to let energies settle.
James never returned for another -
but rang back after I left a message that another massage
sealing light of his spinal cord was needed.
On his saying he 'wasn't having anything to do with that,'
I had to send the sealing through spiritual wires.
And what a bugger Ra turned out to be
in making me think that James would appreciate Mugsy's
Shirley Valentine at the Hole in the Wall.
I'd seen it before and, considering her

the utter explication of the best in zest for living,
thought James might love this red-blooded performance.
But what a deluded ninny I was!
He could barely contain his impatience to be off!
Leaping up during a scene change, which made me leap, too,
we rushed outside into the auditorium.
When it was obvious an act hadn't ended we returned -
slinking sheepishly into seats at the back!
After this mismatched partnering, James asked me back
for tea and fruit at his father's salubrious apartment
overlooking the river in South Perth.
Sipping the tea, he said he hadn't enjoyed
Miss Muggleford's performance, considering
any actress portraying a 'woman like that'
must be either a low-down scrubber or a high-class broad.
But his opinion may have been coloured
by his father's taste for highfalutin party popsies!
Anyway, it was hardly surprising when dropping
upon me unexpectedly one night to request I read his tarot -
(becoming more than a mite impatient
when it took the High Priestess hours!)
that, when leaving, he pulled back
when I forwardly puckered a parting peck for his cheek!
Wavering at the door, his tarot half read,
James wafted friendship in the wind as to whether
this multi-talented, yet dubious female might be feared

for attempting an unsolicited kiss to his cheek.
And what a cheek he had the night he popped round
unsolicited (when I'd specifically told him
to phone up first) and, pulling my lounge chairs apart, he
directly faced me to reverently discuss
the cost of Persian carpets,
and whether air-coolers might keep a heap of chocolate cool.
Keeping my cool, I offered
'why not talk instead about yourself,'
which pulled him apart, making him leap up and out of my life -
much to Ra's chagrin but my satisfaction,
seeing at last the foolishness of fooling
with good-looking though otherwise lacking men.
Ah sweet youth, and the adolescent who versified then
about blue park benches and how life's a kind of lolly -
suck it and taste the sweetness of worms?
Then there's that frosty quote
Rex smote me with the night we met:
'The woods are lovely, dark and deep,
but I have promises to keep -
and miles to go before I sleep.'
Haven't we all? But Rex covered a few that day
when he and Lucy shone it to Mum that I was schizoid -
or was at least exhibiting the classic symptoms!
And didn't I know my tigers and whales were only
shards to shade my eyes from the world's lunacy!

But musing over my fractured experience with men,
I was amused when Ainslie (she of the light and dreamy
    touch,)
called to tell me of her many experiences
of the baffling sex, finding (in her former profession)
how they varied - desiring either the whip,
or a whimsical lavishing of all the affection
she could offer in a steamy hot bath!
That brought back a sunbeam of a memory!
Well, see you when I summon a tiger or two
to stuff in my tank, and zoom off to find the man
who bathed me like a babe. Bye.

GRIEF I USED TO HUG BUT NOW HOLD SACRED

Hugging private grief, I shed my tears alone.
Borne to the mountain, I spend the days
surrendering my will. Finally released
from fear, new life awaits
to receive indictments of love.

OSSIE EMU AND HIS CRICKET TEAM (MARK 1)

Ossie emu had a dream,
which was to form a cricket team.
He set about it with a will,
choosing players great in skill
defending Australia from the Yanks,
the Turks, the Irish and certain banks,
which, lavishly endowing cash,
enticed them all to join the lash -
men who normally wouldn't mix with crew
that daily stoushed them on to brew
the beer that Bondy stews -
but then, I never read the news -
and don't intend to muck abart
by tracing guys who fart
around the base of trees,
hoping eventually to freeze
quantities of other liquor -
like federal policy - changing quicker
than truth or meaning in the dog-star's eye,
sent here solely, I believe, to spy
out one who stays at home,
and doesn't leave her flat to roam ...
but hang on, why not say this out?
Rex (he who hopes to lose his gout)
has promised to delve, nay - come up with
the answer to my pith,

no, plight ... yes, that's what
he said ... wait, no, I only thought that
what he uttered was how he hated
my poems and plays on words, because they rated
with hatters, and loony creatures,
who (unlike him) never scorned to blow features -
noses, rather, I mean to say,
but hang on, let me play
the fool deeper and wider
than he who, parading his little Cider ...
that's me, of course - just call me Rosie
(how often did I blow his nosey?)
But when I learned how easily men
kick scruples aside when trying to ken
a way of getting into my parlour ...
what I mean is, he who learns the art
of loving too late - lacks ardour!
Oops. Now I've really made a muck up -
Perhaps I'll try to straighten this mess,
or better still, do nothing less
than type this tripe, knowing it's crazy
but how silly when the one called Daisy
told me once that she'd make a pattern
which would please my mum - and she's no slattern.
Wait on, what I mean to say
is why don't you begin each day
by rhyming words and singing
trees, up to their roots ... no, leaves, in winging

birds - who praise themselves a great deal better
than people who think they know what letter,
or is it number, making a two-by-four? ...
But you needn't think I'm out the door,
or yet up my tree. I'm told to please
myself a whole heap in loving trees.
Though now, each night and day
when beating, no, braying
my drum, when trying to queen my way
into stony hearts who never say
'Hi, Robsie, how's it going?'
Look! Why not end right here, and find a rowing
boat to push abart a bit
in? Bugger! I'm never a hit
these days with that rotten crumb,
Bob, who promised once to come
and get it! And that's not all -
my Rex never calls
since I chucked him out ...
and a wonderful lout
he was that day in Kings Park
when Ra's spiritual gold made its mark -
for mindfully stealing away
I tricked him a treat by playing
up, and turned on the flow
of the good King Wenceslas ... no,
does Ra think I'm senseless? Why not slur,
no, write my own words, and purr

my part the way that ghost
who commands I say 'mine host,'
and 'my queen,' when Ra, no Sheer Khan I mean
(she who's much too holy to lean
on trunks of old clothes) - as do paper tigers,
who, mewling and mewing, never lie
gracefully down to spiritual efficacy of raw gold,
but rue the king whale who, holding
royal court, effects new-world lores,
where obsolete, archaic wars
between those playing parts
on many stages, need crave only their heart's
desire ... but isn't that the way
the world's made in a single day
when the sun is shining, and gold forthcoming?
But how could I possibly know about that? For bumming
about on paper stages,
I only wage war on pages
of riven gold ... no, what I mean
is, now my heart is clean
and bright since the pulping of roses
and I'm constantly blowing my own and other's noses -
I'll never be forced into blowing the whistle,
not on flute, or lyre, or animal's pizzle -
nor will I have to pull the plug,
or, in depression, stoush my own mug -
for why cease loving this beautiful earth,
when it's stuffed with sods and people of worth?

Unstoppered hearts, tell me, you who've won peace
where can I find it - that golden fleece?

OSSIE EMU AND HIS CRICKET TEAM (MARK 2)

Ossie emu had a dream,
which was to form a cricket team.
He set about it with a will,
and chose his players with great skill.
Say on, said Ossie, shout it out,
men who would so blindly flout
the ashes, and rout the earth
by stifling the birth
of nations, should gird their loins,
for now I've seen the coins
of reason, I haven't a doubt
we'll successfully rout
those hopeful luggers away of the green
and gold - men who only preen
their feathers, and say they'll stew
our guts for garters, but never do
anything, knowing that the good Lord
loves us - so why not board
the buggers and thank the one
who delivered to the world his only son,
and blesses us daily, both early and late?
Clearly, he's rated
the best, for baking bread
that's unleavened, those who haven't a red
cent, and are most in need,
receive daily cake. He says we must heed

our hearts and heads, that reason and love
may combine - not conflict! So let's hove
to and get on with plain living -
instead of striving
to achieve gold and green
with that cup, weaning
ourselves from the love of the mother
who never bush-whacks us - or others
for playing up late -
(as I did once) but wait
a mo, why not write this myself
instead of scribing for Pinkerton - that tiresome elf
who said I'd never find spiritual gold
at my core ... no, hold
on, perhaps you'd like to search for your centre?
Or, to put it another way, go find your mentor? -
he who helps us to see when we look,
so instead of just screwing our eyes in a book,
or chewing our nails right down to the nub ...
Hang on, why don't I state the hub
of things spiritual and say
all that's needed when going for the pay-
out in raw gold, is just to play
up, and muck abart, the way
I'm told to these days,
by Ra, Tigger, and that cool cat Sheer ... hey!
They're lying to me again!
Just let me get my ... wait, Ben -

yes, he who said I'd be
a mother once more, now that one, no, three
tricky bastards who wish me well -
yet treat me so meanly ... 'Go to hell!'
(Just me bawling out mine host)
what's he, no, she ... bugger! What the ghost ...
What I mean is, whenever I muck up,
Ra refuses to let me pucker up
and offer anew
these lips that are long overdue
for a kiss from him who never says 'please.'
But no, for strafing and teasing,
he'd only torment me ...
Why aren't I ever allowed to be
merely myself? Wait a mo,
'why' - that's what I sow
too often in Ra's tawny lug - and what a muck-up
our marriage, no, poem is! 'Ruck,
Robsie, rots of ruck,' - that's what a friend
said, knowing I penned
a letter, most cryptic, to Joanne
who I never knew well in the days we began
to ruck up, by writing loads of this
shit - for instance my version of hell, with Dis
its landlord ... no words
can describe that stasher of goats, that herder
who ... wait - I've made a muckle once more ...
Time to shut up shop and bore

you no more. Look - in lieu
of all this, why not read how the ewe
scored a hit when the zodiac cricket team
bore away gold of a different seam?
not unlike gold I'm having to strive
for by killing my ego, which, like a hive
of fleas, wasn't the knees-up
Ra said it would be, after heaving up
my breath for the body and soul
of this world (holding up, as a symbol, a vase of whole
white light.) And 'well done!' -
that's what I said when I won -
after braving the whole damned bunch
who, each and every one, just longed to punch
me one on the snout,
for, acting the Christ, they wanted to clout
me. Why? Every one in this world's
no different than me … so if you think I've hurled
myself into the pitch of Ra's making
you need a good waking
up. Both Tiger Burning Brightly
and Sheer Khan day and nightly
say pleasing myselves and me
paves the way to gold, so let's see …
time to queen it up on stages
greener than a lemon crispy. Pages
ago Ra wrote that. My green's
to be delivered by that blackest of queens,

Raw Gold |247

Sheer Shit. So what if these clawing cats tease -
it's pleasing squeezing fleas!

OSSIE EMU AND HIS CRICKET TEAM (MARK 3)

Ossie emu had a dream
which was to form a cricket team.
He set about it with a will
and chose his players with great skill:
Ken koala, Sam the skink,
Wally wombat - in the pink,
Barry bat (who came much later)
and Rodney roo, whose fame was greater
than any of that stalwart crew.
Hotly debating their rival team, 'chew
their ears off,' said Sam the skink,
and Wally wombat said, 'I think
our team will do quite well,
if only we give them hell
for leather … yes, that's it
we'll score a hit
and tell our captain news
of the team which mews
and crows and pleads for mercy …'
We'll show 'em none, now Percy,
he who was named
a silly coot and blamed
by those in hallowed halls for yelling 'shoot,'
or was it 'root
my socks off!' Don't heed my words -
he called that team 'stupid nerds,'

then, effing and blinding, beat a hasty retreat.
Ra lies - but I'll have to eat
his words and tell how I really came
to lark it up in seas of flame -
which pushed the pitcher off his perch!
Amazed, he lurched,
and fell for my story - and then how I gave him merry hell
for failing to climb down that dinky well -
where Ra and the other three,
(that is to say, myselves and me)
told him to hide in, when playing the fool …
Those ridiculous games would cool
anyone's ardour, and I'm no exception, for Ra
has driven me much too far -
he'll overstep the mark one day,
then I'll flip my lid the way
real loonies do -
and won't that put him in the poo
with Sheer Khan? - She's on my side
(or was,) and knowing I long for a ride
in a park that's not blue,
has promised me horses of regular hue.
I'd like to give Ra a piece of my mind -
no, let him take the lot. I can't even find
a small space to think, free from his prying eye -
there's no cranny, or nook that's private
these days. My head rattles with chatter,
and nattering endlessly, he asks what's the matter

when I threaten to tear snake, owl and gorilla from their
    stand,
when pushed much too far by his constant demand
that I listen, take note, and do
exactly what he tells me to.
How I long for the freedom to go where I choose,
or ring certain friends without Ra's strict refuse.
Locked away in my flat, I get bloody lonely,
and frequently wish oh if only, if only
the one I adore would get his head read
for refusing to see me - the tears I have shed
would fill a hot bath -
but the great Ra himself can't make Bob beat a path
to my door. What a sucker
I was to think luck - or
at least my fortune had changed
when Ra rambled and ranged
as he scrambled my mind
with belief that I'd find
absolute happiness, joy - even bliss
with he who once kissed
me. Sharing intimate thoughts
that night, I never guessed how mortified
I'd feel when, for no reason
other than kicking in my teeth one winter season,
he totally rejected me. I endure now a spinsterish state,
as all the men in my life HATED
the way I prated of Ra, Sheer and Tigger -

not to mention Adonis, Apollo and Sirius -
men just couldn't figure
their rating so highly -
but those sly wily
bastards dig in their claws,
and pad round my head on their soft paddy paws,
then trick me and treat me,
confound and defeat me,
till let down and lost, confused and abused,
I'm clay for their kneading, and just not amused.
Having got to rock bottom, through searing in hell,
and suffered the torments, till broken, my will
I relinquished - no longer that free
happily autonomous creature, gaily gadding about and
larking it up on this mad-cap planet, the me
I've become since conceived by these cats
is a multiple-divinitied, highly complex -
yet extremely simple being that
just needs a tiny quantity of pure unadulterated love
to survive in this world. Heavens above!
You'd think I'd got the plague! You won't catch
your death coming near me - snatch
a moment to hug, hold and love me
to death for life. Phone, tee
up a time to come round and see me. Be
my friend, pal, lover - but don't reject me again, for never
    again do I want to be so LONELY!

MY PATE ON A PLATTER

Inviting me in for tea and fruit,
the grinning face leered its last
tear-stained, glaring sin. Suiting myself,
I ate the fruit, downed a mug or two
of bitter tea, and left.
None the wiser, I wept for an unknown sin.

THE UNKNOWN MAN

The one I'm yet to meet
daily passes me in the street.
The one I'm yet to know
fondly supposes I grow wiser
than once when, desiring,
we touched, reaching for each other
with all the love we knew.
Quiescently I wait to meet the one
I'm yet unable to know.

THE SPORT OF KINGS

Happiness, I've found, is never gained
through self-confession. Now my poor heart
sinks whenever the men I know
misinterpret swords which pierce them.
Raw gold, driven from all foreign matter,
is never found in icy hearts. Now kings (like Rex)
play foolish games of tennis, and knees-up
with mother, (who never plays games, or even
shows much interest in the sport of kings.)
Times healthier than these, in which
our future kings raise rackets to beat
those driving steel wedges into hearts of flesh,
will act from souls and hearts of riven gold.

TALES TO TELL MOTHER

Telling mother I am mad, Lou-lou exploded silences,
secrets kept a lifetime.
Straightening my shawl, I took bouquets of flowers,
bequeathing boundless joy upon the heart
of her who loves me well.
Blowing out the flame of fearful tongues,
mum drew me to her breast
and heaved a sigh of deep relief.
'Welcome, welcome back,' she beamed.
'Your son has returned,' I said.

BALD PATES AND SAVAGE FELINES

Pleasing myself, I pleased the one
who loved me least. Dull-hearted,
he squirmed and wriggled in his chair,
until wormish sighs squiggled
across aeons of grievous pages.
The sage grew silent. Then suddenly,
'stand up and write, you silly sod,' he said.
Then I saw him as he was: a balding king
who queened away his days, banqueting
in palaces where knights, armed with tennis racquets,
play games, and grow greedy to win.

SONG OF DEATH

Desiring peace, desiring to be alone,
I lied to one who loves his life,
and lied to the friend who,
licking his lips, tasted salt fish.
I lied to myself, believing life
a lovely dream, a house of cards
which collapse the pain of being,
without knowing or seeing why.

CHAPTER 12

OPENING MY ARMS TO BLUE HORSES

Considering the chariness most men have in accepting
that physical reality isn't all there is,
and that spirit plays its part in shaping
realities not readily apparent, women -
who for aeons have borne men's derision -
prove their sex's wisdom in seeking to gain
fulfilment in their lives through spirit,
and its guidance towards a unity with the one
who loves our human frailty, and desires
we strengthen our hearts by heeding the wisdom
in their cry. During my time of searing,
undergoing transformation
within the whale's belly, only women
stayed to make the spiritual leap towards
their conscious knowing, by continuing
consultations and enduring all the shrieks,
barks, howls, and a terrifying range
of shooshes, whoops, tonal variations,
and Ra's capricious method
of transferring energy, by his chucking
my body around in such an unseemly
and seemingly crazy manner.
First and foremost of these women is Anne,
a wonderful motherly person
who first came to see me for Touch for Health,
and got much more than all its skills

when told that Hermes Trismegistus,
a giant in intellect who brought medicine,
art, astrology and magic to the world
of the Egyptians, and known by them a god,
said that through aeons, she'd been
'crucified upon the cross of others,
and now must free herself to follow
the pathway of her soul.' For too long
Anne's been burdened by those she cares for,
never allowing herself more than moments
snatched from being a kind of universal mother,
taking on troubles of the world -
and never making time available
for the simple pleasure of enjoying her roses,
or going where her heart delights
instead of hearing only duty's dictates
to fill her day with chores for those she loves -
so disregarding her heart and soul's desires.
Regarding irregularities in the energies
pervading and surrounding Anne, shown through
psychic means to be deficient, I used
a variety of crystals to strengthen and smooth
jagged patches - thus sharpening her inclination
to spend what cash she had to spare
on multi-coloured crystal eggs: a full basket,
filling her eyes with the radiance of their fire.
And Lyn, also fired to walk the path of spirit,
uses crystals, carrying them about her person

for their harmonising power, and way
their energy lifts her spirit.
In a rite of passage once,
she'd played the Christ, praying to God
in the garden of Gethsemane,
while I was a sleeping disciple,
snoring while my Lord bore his suffering alone.
My dear friend, Georgy, too, underwent a ritual with me
by drinking the water of life to regain her soul,
which she said she'd lost when Roger,
her best beloved child, killed her cat.
As a result of this barbaric act
she'd felt disconnected from her soul,
but knew her son's love for her was greater
than her love for the cat.
Ra says I mustn't stay awake too long
in my hell's kitchen, drinking the brew bai lin.
And as beer's an allergy for me
I mustn't drink Bond's brew for some weeks yet.
But moderation, eh? Don't you go stinking
your breath away in bags, and bating your souls
to plug your licences up now will you.
And about Bob, I haven't the ghost of a chance
of silvering up his soul in my arms,
as he's maybe gone away from Mosman Park
to tart it up by spidering with other women.
I didn't like that much when he told me he would,
so I said I, too, would play in other parks.

But what I really meant was
'hold me tighter than a tiger's spring,
and bring me roses grown in snow
to gild my lily.' I still think it a disgrace
for one so clean to scrape
and scrape away the dirt on his fingers
when he'd only been gardening
the day I popped in to see him.
Bob scraped his fingers till they nearly bled,
as my elbow did the night I bathed him
cleaner than a postman's whistle, to whistle up
his female soul, and stopper up his mum
from bleeding him to death.
To-roo, see you soon. I've got to go
and lark it up in other parks. Up the Mossies.
I hope they bite his bum. No, what I mean is
Lucy, who's finally consented to wend her way
to my hell's kitchen for a meal,
gave me a meal from her kitchen once, and very nice
it was too. Toodle-pip. Oops.
Just in case you think we may overdo the wine again,
and get sodden in our cups, then whine about the way
we lose our cash when clutches on cars break up
we'll heed what Ra says and go easy on the wine.
To-roo again. See you in a horses' whinny.
I've got to trowel up some new muck
to chuck in my eye. Bye.

AMAZING AMAZONS

Amazing Amazons, sharing
my desire to thaw out icy hearts,
shed tears of joy when lovers
feel new warmth. Forbidden fruit,
succulent and sweet, spill
secret memories of nights
of stolen bliss, releasing
seeds of woe.
Blessed by women who share
my joy and grief,
I prise open hearts
to discover gold.

LONG LIVE THE QUEENS

Southern islanders, dreaming their youth
in blissful fragrance of heralding smoke,
seek to break decrees of famous men
who seal the fate of ancient lands.
Those spiriting their dreams, send
joyous and triumphant news: the king is dead,
long live the new queens.

GEORGINA AND THE WHITE ANTS (MARK 1)

Georgina and the white ants,
sitting on the floor,
Georgy poked their hollow log
and pushed some out the door.

The white ants cried for mercy,
Georgy said 'no way,'
the white ants went and bit her toes,
which made her scream and say:

'No white ants for dinner,
no white ants for tea,
no white ants for ever more,
I'll make them go away.'

She fetched a heavy rolling pin,
and rolled it up and down,
she rolled it all around the room,
she rolled it into town.

The people, when they saw her
upon her hands and knees,
thought she was not crazy -
just maddened by a breeze

which blew the women's skirts up,
showing their underwear,
(some men had their hats blown off
which made them curse and swear.)

Georgy loved the wind and rain,
she loved the stormy day,
she loved her heavy rolling pin
which rolled the ants away.

She got up slowly from her knees,
then laughed and sang 'hooray,
no more white ants in my pants,
I'll go home now and play.'

GEORGINA AND THE WHITE ANTS (MARK 2)

Georgina and the madman, sitting on the grass,
Georgy bashed a hollow log, and sent him off to class.
Out marched two soldier ants, who shot that madman dead,
and Georgy said 'oh, wicked ones, you've blown off his head.'
Whatever will become of me? I don't know where to go,
there's no one home to comfort me, I cannot even show
the ladies in my yoga class (who'd understand my plight,)
this little sore upon my leg … so maybe I was right
to try to go and lance it, but that stirred bitter dregs,
I think I'll have to chance it, and clean my toothy pegs …
So now I've dumped him in the sea, will anybody care?
They'd surely never blame me, for cleaning up the air -
'cos what a rotten stink he'd make, if left there to decay,
I had to do it right away - no reason for delay …
but what if now I draw the ire of madmen everywhere?
Their awful fangs, and wandering hands, proved more than I could bear,
when last I looked upon his kith (and some of them were kin,)
… so when he tried to kith me, I thought it such a sin,
I had to go and find my gun - a toy one, to be sure -
I know there was no harm in it, I never thought the law
would break my breath and grind my bones - all because I said,
'oh, wicked me, I went and shot that rotten madman dead.'

FOR GEORGINA

Lessons I must learn concern myselves and me.
I love myself three times whalely;
I will not expect others to love me daily -
unless I am a wonderful whale.
I must not mistake myself
for she who never allowed herself
to be truly herselves.
Never have I been more beautiful
than I am right now - or known a better me.
Only now, when summer is a coming in,
am I pleased to say 'I love myselves and me,'
because now I love myself
more than the being
who once displeased me so.

GEORGINA THE GREEN

Georgy has no more white ants in her pants,
because she quietly governs beings who leave
their fibrous waste upon her floors,
and play up, by eating out her kitchen drawers.
Now, she never lets annoyance show,
but mildly rids her house of pests.
Silver-paper balls of glittering light reflect
her future, as brightly flickering candles,
borne upon the backs of blue humped whales,
draw her on to be new-named. Soon all
will know her as Georgina the Green,
a beautiful soul, whose hands tend winter roses,
whiter than newly-blanketed snow,
which shed their petals on the frozen earth,
and releasing perfume, alert the gods,
soon to govern her. Then a power,
blessed by doves of peace, who love her
as do summer whales for grace she bears the earth,
will spiral in, ridding the remnants of grief.
Let joy fulfil her days when heaven
sets ablaze her rings of ice,
to grace and further green her soul.

CHAPTER 13

BLUE SPIRIT POLES AND OTHER ART WORKS

When whistling in the dark the night I died,
I harried up a host of demons who pricked my soul.
Then realising I'd died only to myself
I got back up on my blue horse,
determined to ride where love alone led.
Loving Gordon well, despite having left him,
I telephoned Rachael, asking her to ask her father
to see a doctor, as I knew no way
he'd have Touch for Health from me.
She slammed down the phone - as I think
I've mentioned before - and when I called back
a few minutes later, she told me
never to include either of them again
in absentia Touch for Health. All very well,
but much comes unsolicited by my whales,
or whoever happens to be talking at the time,
and I feel an awesome responsibility
to pass the information on. But in their case,
never, never again! I wish both
Gordon and Rachael bounteous health and happiness.
And for myself, better communication
with them both. But as Rachael's
put the kibosh on that, clearly stating
that she'll resume her relationship
with me 'after settlement,' there's nothing
I can do but wait. And wait, and wait.

Waiting seems to be the state of the arts.
How many blue days and nights must I pass
to be guided more greenly in love. How much
experience will it take to drain the blue,
leaving a brighter and healthier hue. Give me
red-blooded days, that the art of the state
may thrive, and fill my life with love,
blossoming greenly in scarlet roses.
But till then, wait I must for Bob
to see if he'll ever change his heart and mind
and ring me up ... I wonder if Sheila,
she who in matters of Anatomy and Physiology
must always be obeyed, has barked him up
any good gum trees lately.
'You've got to be joking,' Bob cried once
from the topmost branches. 'I'm not
going to break a leg, or any other part
for that matter - especially my heart.
It'll never wear its flip-flops, no, pants
for you, to tear to bits of bone and bum.'
But once he tore my burning part from its chest,
and flung it panting in the kitchen sink.
He wouldn't even let me wipe his dishes,
or mop his floor when I begged him
let me visit again. I must be bonkers
to love this loony. Can't he see the value
of unrequited love streaming from my eyes?
But though I keep telling God I want a kind man,

one who'd love me in return, I'm constantly told
'seek no further than Bob McCloud.'
Mine is not to wonder why, it seems,
but when the doing and the dying
grow tedious through repetition,
God grant me strength not to seek
love's silver lining in Bob McCloud's
dark looks. Oh for a dog to love
and take for walks. As I'm lying in this park,
gnawing an apple, and boning up
on the whys and wherefores
of love's labours lost, Hannah, a boxer dog,
prances by, full of spring
and the delight of taking her mistress
for a walk. A tiny tear pricks my eye
remembering a childhood that was dog-enriched.
Flossy, where are you now? Have you
transmigrated? How I'd care for you,
love and cherish you free of arthritis and fleas
if I had you now. But the luxury of dog days
are beyond me. No pets in flats -
and when I do move to some kind of housette,
will I buy a dog to tie me down to walks
and vets? Better to pat the odd stray
and stay away from canine and cat owners'
responsibilities. I'll take myself for walks
to the river. Or go with a friend.
I took Ainslie for a walk there recently,

and she filled my ear with new-age talk about outsides
    mirroring insides.
I liked it better when she told of more vainglorious days
when working as a prostitute. 'I received
high acclaim,' she recalled, 'for having
the imagination to keep a client entertained
the whole night through.' Hard cash and acclaim!
As a masseuse now she's paid well for extras.
Life's a soggy weet-bix. I'm too straight-laced
for extras. God, how about just the main course?
Come January when I've been rebirthed, will life be any
    better as a new Christ?
Will God find me a new man to love, or will I need to
    live out my life alone,
grateful for the love of friends?
Yours in love and art, Robin. Bye.

REAPING HAVOC'S HARVEST

Starry dogs who carry treasure to troves
that pleasure strives to please, beckon to one
who, immured in hell, arises to slither
down a crow's nest which, hither to, offered
a good long look at twenty years of a happy marriage,
yet currently shows the clarity of clear confusion.
Here from the poop, I see that Gordon,
First Mate aboard the H.M.A.S. Scrimpbank,
pitching through seas greener than pea-chunder,
hurled by he who thunders mayhem's havoc
from the sky, needs hearken
to his heart's insistent cry. Whaling up
my long-dead dog to while away love's pride,
we catch a linnet by the wing, hoping for a song
from Rachael to fill our hearts with joy. Stony stares,
and swords which pierce the side, slide
agonising dreams in a mind which, freewheeling,
and reeling in the sun of one magnanimous and wise,
is overwhelmed with wonder. Gazing dreamily
towards the west, I muse on lives which,
split asunder, drop their leaves,
before rising sap once more sends buds
to drink the rain and sun, and blossom forth
their rainbow colours, blissful in the one
who shares divinity. But now I wait on starry dogs
to guide me blindly to my love, now smitten

with an unknown blight, and blossom joys
to blaze our contradictory hearts.

PALACE RELIEF

A masseuse of many talents,
Ainslie brought her clients
great relief from tensions,
and the pressures
of angry jaundiced palaces -
places where they gently
played the goat,
and acted up.

A RIPPING GOOD TIME

Faintly bored, Ainslie sighed,
and whisked another fly.
Blowing out the light, she said,
'right, fine, discipline it is.'
Her client, lusting after blood,
placed himself entirely in her hands.
She oiled her breasts,
painted daggers on her arms,
and, scorning the man
who paid her price,
took up the whip.
Wilting, lily-livered, he longed
for the lash, the barbarous joy
of flagellation's ripped flesh.
Ainslie raised the whip,
and brought it down
upon a wooden stool.

THORNY TOAD

Driven to humiliating shame,
the queen's toad lusted for revenge.
Lately he'd only seemed
to wear the thorny girdle.
Naked, he circled the hall.
His paunch sagged to his knees.
Haunches lean and crouched,
he danced a toady waltz.
The queen, pointing a slender finger,
desired he quicken his pace.
Faster and faster danced the toad.
Angered by his silence,
the queen bid him croak sins.
Obsequiously the toad hopped forward.
'Croak-croak, croak-croak,' he cried,
then wrung her neck.

REPTILE BRIDES

The lizard queen, curving the post
of her king's pride, employed
desiring arms to charm her drunken lord.
Raging silently, she scorned
foolish brides who lightly unfurl
their mysteries, wishing for spears
with which to pierce their sides.

MUSINGS ON LOVE

Androgyny, beloved of the muse,
fidgets in his sleep, confusing
pain with joy's steep ungainly heights.
Plummeting to depths, he seeks power
to rise, and queen it with kings.

THE INS AND OUTS OF LOVE

The wages of sin are not to go in,
but soak to the skin in a storm,
for if I go in, no sin-bin awaits my lust -
just a worm's-eye view of death.
In storms I have known, my scruples have shown
that I am the one who will die,
and now having grown in love so forlorn,
I always stay in when it storms,
writing screeds about love - but never getting any.
In stepping over the hurdle of words
that stagnate and curdle my brain,
I submit to purging when it rains,
and allow it to pour on my head.

SUBSONIC GRIEF (MARK 1)

Fate holds no terrors now of death
for, making my way to stars
mid pain and pleasure,
I face eternal life.

SUBSONIC GRIEF (MARK 2)

Awesome events, rising with labouring whales,
manifest through death's dark floor.
Calling across blue radiance, they sing
of broken gyres which tilt towards past suns.
Braiding golden strands of winter fire,
I wait to erase the grief of aeons,
and cool my raging mind.

DOG STAR VISIONS

Brilliant stars pulsate their light
through skies of black, signalling a birth.
Sirius brings new life on earth.
Death's winding sheets hide ashen clouds,
scoring sparks across deserted beaches.
Sands, grey with dust, blow
crazy patterns in smoke-blackened skies.

LITTLE GIRL LOST

A photograph of myself at seventeen
shows the loneliness of a little girl lost.
I was sweeter then than she who now demands
her way, pushing and shoving in hearts and bones,
bullying clients to better health.
However, the life I lead right now is treasured,
and ancient mariners, fishing from my depths
the pearl of wisdom, draw me to distant lands
on seas of fire. Breaking seals, I prophesy
an age when the New World Order, whose crew -
featured in akashic catalogues - help certify
the deal when January the eighth, when I'm reborn,
hastens me back to find
that the sons and daughters of Calgary
are not lost, but merely dreaming.

BREAKING THE SEALS

January comes a blowing in
to stir desiring hearts,
which ne'er do well in searing hells,
when kings and queens of tarts
trade off miracles
against their reasoning minds.
When hot summer winds reek
with the stench of war,
promises of a new-born passion -
woven in gold and silver tapestry -
pledge peace with tribes
who spend their days in grief,
believing the ancient lie:
half a life is better than no bread.
Rhythms drummed upon the burning log
drive worldly fears in hearts of woe.
Blessed are they who, trading
old lamps for new, break ancient seals
to discover they are kings and queens
of a glorious New World Order.

THE END

ABOUT THE AUTHOR

Born in Subiaco and growing up in Bunbury, my first job was as junior typist with a firm of solicitors. I then worked in a bank, followed by the Department of Agriculture.

I had always wanted to be an actor so I joined the Bunbury Repertory Company where I played in 'Charley's Aunt', 'Simon and Laura' and was 'Ado Annie' in 'Oklahoma' at the Bunbury Musical Comedy Group.

I then lived for a year in Melbourne and joined the staff of the ABC. I played Jan in Alan Seymour's 'One Day of the Year' at the Arrow theatre. Back in Perth, I worked in the ABC before going to England to get married. I worked in a number of offices at the BBC in London and joined the Studio Amateur Dramatic Group where I acted in a number of radio plays and won Actress of the Year in 1968.

I came back to Perth in 1968 and my daughter was born in 1969. I worked in Sound Effects at the Perth

ABC until 1980 and joined the Actors' Company where I played in 'Wings', 'Ring Around the Moon' and 'Uncle Vanya' and took a poetry program to a number of schools. I also played in a greenroom production of the National Theatre.

As my acting career hadn't really taken off, I started writing theatre reviews for the Daily News, and then for a bi-monthly magazine called New Theatre Australia. By this time I had completed my BA degree in Creative Writing at Curtin University, which I did part-time, and I found that the frequent late nights were taking their toll.

My marriage broke up in 1988 and I experienced schizophrenia the following year. It was lucky I had studied Touch for Health, (or Kinesiology as it is now called) as it helped me to understand my spiritual journey and has kept me in balance for the last thirty or so years.